ECONOMICS AND PUBLIC POLICY

THE BROOKINGS INSTITUTION

The Brookings Institution is an independent organization engaged in research and education in the social sciences. Its principal purposes are to aid in the development of sound public policies and to provide advanced training for students in the social sciences.

The Institution was founded December 8, 1927 as a consolidation of three antecedent organizations: the Institute for Government Research, 1916; the Institute of Economics, 1922; and the Robert Brookings Graduate School of Economics and Government, 1924.

The general administration of the Institution is the responsibility of a self-perpetuating Board of Trustees. In addition to this general responsibility the By-Laws provide that, "It is the function of the Trustees to make possible the conduct of scientific research and publication, under the most favorable conditions, and to safeguard the independence of the research staff in the pursuit of their studies and in the publication of the results of such studies. It is not a part of their function to determine, control, or influence the conduct of particular investigations or the conclusions reached." The immediate direction of the policies, program, and staff of the Institution is vested in the President, who is assisted by an advisory council, chosen from the professional staff of the Institution.

In publishing a study the Institution presents it as a competent treatment of a subject worthy of public consideration. The interpretations and conclusions in such publications are those of the author or authors and do not necessarily reflect the views of other members of the Brookings staff or of the administrative officers of the Institution.

ECONOMICS
and
PUBLIC POLICY

Brookings Lectures, 1954

ARTHUR SMITHIES JOHN JEWKES

JOSEPH J. SPENGLER JACOB VINER

FRANK H. KNIGHT LIONEL ROBBINS

THE BROOKINGS INSTITUTION

Washington, D.C.

1955

Printed in the United States of America
George Banta Publishing Company
Menasha, Wisconsin

Foreword

THE BROOKINGS LECTURES were inaugurated in 1954 to advance research in the social sciences. For this initial series, six distinguished economists were invited to discuss various aspects of policy as a concern of economics. The audience consisted mainly of social scientists in government, in neighboring institutions, and from the Brookings staff.

The theme of these lectures relates directly to the objectives of the Brookings Institution, which are to advance knowledge and understanding of economic and political problems, both national and international, and of the courses of action that may be pursued in dealing with them. The purpose of the Institution in advancing knowledge and understanding is to facilitate the making of informed decisions in the public interest on matters of general concern.

This emphasis on research for the guidance of action involves considerably more than a concern with immediate problems and the application of existing knowledge. Although the investigation of current problems must go on, the larger task is to advance the use of the social sciences in the rational conduct of social affairs.

Economic analysis has come to have an important influence on policy and the daily conduct of affairs. The use of economics in analyzing problems for decision can be greatly improved by (a) a better understanding of economics and its application to policy problems, (b) improvements in economic concepts, theories, and methods, (c) improvements in the arts of research for the guidance of action, and (d) a better understanding of contemporary social processes by both professional students and the general public. By advances of this sort, the potential benefits of economic analysis may be more fully realized.

These lectures discuss economics and its application to policy problems. They examine, in turn, economic welfare as an objective of policy, the contribution that economic theory may make to public policy, the central place of freedom, order, and justice as objectives in a changing world, the economist's responsibilities, the relevance of international trade theory, and a further examination of the relation between freedom and order and their policy implications.

Together, these lectures present a useful review of economic thinking with respect to the utilization of economics for the guidance of action. They help to orient the reader with respect to past achievements and to delineate the areas where further effort may be fruitful. The task of perfecting and enlarging scientific knowledge of economic life is endless. Great advances in economic thinking have been made, and these accomplishments of the past should not be underestimated. Yet clearly, there lie ahead urgent and challenging opportunities for the further development of economics as a means to better understanding and to the formulation of rational policy.

The Brookings Lectures were established by the Brookings Institution with the support of Mrs. Robert S. Brookings. To her, the Institution is especially indebted for the gift that permitted the inauguration of this series of lectures, and even more for the vision and faith that have characterized her interest in measures to improve the conduct of public affairs.

ROBERT D. CALKINS
President

December 1954

Contents

Contents

1

Economic Welfare and Policy

ARTHUR SMITHIES[1]

ECONOMICS HAS ALWAYS been concerned with policy. Most economists have been motivated by the desire to promote what they considered to be social improvement—Cournot, Walras, and Schumpeter are among the few eminent exceptions of the past, who come readily to mind. Adam Smith, Ricardo, Mill, Marshall, and Keynes fall just as readily into the category of economists with strong policy motivations. Whatever the motivation of the economist, most economic analysis has strong policy implications. The general equilibrium system of Walras, for instance, can be regarded equally as an explanatory instrument and as a prescription of an economic norm for society. The theory provides solid support for the view that an individualistic society can achieve harmonious and desirable economic results.

I

Concern with policy inevitably prevents economics from being or becoming a self-contained compartment of the social sciences. It must be based on ethical or political presuppositions derived from the noneconomic world. One cannot believe in full employment or free trade as desirable economic objectives exclusively on economic grounds. This dependence on the outside world has led economists who object to the incursion of their brethren into the political world or who entertain hopes of making economics "scientific" to urge that

[1] Professor of Economics, Harvard University.

1

economics be stripped of its prescriptions and be confined to matters of analysis.[2]

On this view the policy role of the economist would be to advise on means rather than ends, to point out to the politician the consequences of various alternative courses of action, and to leave the question of value judgments to him. Attractive though this position may appear from some points of view, I do not believe it is tenable for a variety of reasons.

In the first place, hardly any economic theory can be considered ideologically neutral. In fact, the assertion or denial of the objectivity of an economic theory itself implies a value judgment. To illustrate, the analysis of business cycles can hardly be conducted in terms of all fluctuating economic variables. The analyst must select those he considers the most significant. A theory that asserts that the central feature of the business cycle is fluctuations in the employment of labor is likely to convey very different social implications from one which centers attention on fluctuations in bank credit. Yet both theories may be equally valid from the "scientific" point of view. Emphasis on employment, and even more on unemployment, conveys the idea that there is an urgent social problem to be solved, whereas emphasis on monetary factors may create a very different impression—as it did during the nineteenth century. The only neutral way to analyze the business cycle is to discuss everything connected with it. But such a procedure would have little usefulness from an analytic point of view.

In the second place, the mere selection of economic problems for investigation involves value judgments. Despite a surfeit of research money, the human resources for research remain limited. The way in which research activity is allocated among, say, problems of economic growth, business cycles, or

---

[2] Lionel Robbins, *An Essay of the Nature and Significance of Economic Science* (1931); and Gunnar Myrdal, *The Political Element in the Development of Economic Theory* (1954).

the structure of the market affects the policy attention that those matters will receive in the future. Even though the research may be originally undertaken in response to some demand for it, the fruits of the research will influence that demand in the future. At a time when the direction of research is bound to be strongly affected by the deliberate policy of foundations in selecting the type of projects they will finance, a sharp distinction between analysis and its policy implications seems particularly difficult to maintain.

In the third place, attempts to draw sharp distinctions between means and ends can be misleading and dangerous. The means chosen to achieve particular ends today may alter the ends of tomorrow. Although economists—with the notable exception of Frank H. Knight—have chosen to overlook this point for the sake of their analytic structures, the assumption of constant "tastes" is an unwarranted simplification. It is of the essence of the course of economic life of an individual or a nation that ends and means react on each other. Were it not for the fact that supply can create demand, the course of economic development would have been radically different or nonexistent. Where, for instance, would the automobile industry stand today if the human appetite for automobiles were merely what it was half a century ago? To illustrate the same point from the field of public policy: an economist may advise that the cheapest way to get "defense" is to abandon conventional weapons in favor of atomic weapons. But in my opinion he would be irresponsible if he failed to consider the consequences of such a change on the policy objectives of the future.

There is a final and practical reason why the economist—particularly the economic adviser—must concern himself with value judgments. An economic problem of any importance is too complicated for all such judgments involved in its solution to be set out explicitly. An economist who is advising a President on whether or not to employ direct controls in time of inflation must base his advice largely on his views on the importance or the unimportance of preserving a free market economy. Those views necessarily involve value judgments, but Presidents are far too occupied with the urgent issues of the moment to listen to an elaborate dissection of their advisers' viewpoint. In selecting an adviser, the President should make sure that his adviser's views on policy will correspond generally with his own. But he is unlikely to receive much usable advice if the adviser is unwilling to commit himself on policy issues.

Although I insist that the economist cannot perform his function if he persists in sticking to a narrow definition of his last, I do not mean to imply that he should go to the opposite extreme and claim the whole field of social science as his province. The fact that he has to go outside the area of his specialty does not mean that he is an expert in other areas or that there is not abundant room for experts within the field of economics.

Our record in the political field is not particularly impressive. The rationalistic nature of economics has led us to assume too readily that the politicians to whom we recommend action are dominated by rational considerations of the common good. We have ignored the fact that they themselves are at the mercy of the political forces that have placed them in power. Our proposals for economic stability through fiscal and monetary measures might have been substantially different had we realized that some of the most powerful organized groups had little interest in carrying them out. We could have profited from the advice of political scientists—if there are any who are sufficiently impressed with the economic components of political action.

I can illustrate the role I believe the economist should play with respect to policy by an analogy with the role of a medical doctor in his relations with his patient. The doctor must be an expert in medical matters, but I do not see how he can base his advice, in a complicated case, on medical grounds, alone. Before advising the patient to give up smoking or drinking or to alter his way of life in other ways, he must form some notion of what the patient wants out of life. To give up smoking may increase the speed at which the patient can run a mile, but the patient may not have the slightest desire to run at all, and he does have a strong desire to smoke. But the doctor may decide that there is serious conflict between the patient's desire to smoke and his desire to live to the age of seventy. He may then feel no hesitation in using all his authority to make the patient alter his present manner of living. But in doing so he decides, on the basis of his knowledge of the patient, that it is a good thing for the patient to live to a ripe old age and to make some immediate sacrifices in order to do so. The doctor must make such judgments in order to function adequately in his medical capacity. He should not go further and advise the patient on aspects of his life that are unrelated to his medical health. The patient should choose for himself between pushpin and poetry—or else appeal to his hedonistic adviser.

In a similar way, I believe the economist should diagnose and prescribe for society. His function is not to attempt to create a Utopia that conforms to his own predilections. His task is to determine the economic conditions whereby society can realize its aspirations, to recognize that there is continual interaction between the economic means employed and the objectives that a society sets for itself, and to propose changes in those objectives when economic analysis reveals that society may be frustrated through the pursuit of contradictory ends. This function is more adequately indicated by the term "political economy" than by the more scientific "economics."

II

Having asserted the economists' interest in policy, let us now review the approaches to the welfare problem that have been proposed or used by economists during the period from Adam Smith to the present time. To sketch the picture in its broadest outlines and to run the usual risks of name-calling, I propose to distinguish among the Classical, the Pigouvian, the Paretian, and the Keynesian approaches to the welfare problem. Each of these approaches was largely a product of its time, and none of them meets entirely the needs of the present.

The Classical Economists, Adam Smith, Ricardo, and their followers, were prepared to identify welfare with the accumulation of wealth and the consequent increase in output; and in employing these concepts they were not tortured by the doubts that the utility analysis and the reactions from it have aroused. Adam Smith's major contention was that the removal of economic restrictions widens the market, increases the possibilities of the division of labor, and results in an increased accumulation of wealth and output.

While Ricardo was no less concerned than Smith with freedom of trade, his analysis centered around profits as the source of accumulation, and the Malthusian spector added a sense of urgency to the need for accumulation and increased industrial analysis. Virtually all public policies in the economic field could then be approved or condemned by reference to their effects in increasing or diminishing industrial profits. Free trade was good because it reduced the value of real wages and thereby increased the profit margin and the rate of accumulation. All taxes were bad because no tax could fail to diminish profits either directly or indirectly through raising wages. The best tax—probably a tax on rent—was that which had the least adverse effect on profits. An engine of analysis that could produce such quick and conclusive answers to policy questions was not to be seen again until 1936.

While the Classical Economists saw the welfare question in terms of economic growth, their conception of the needs of their times rendered their analysis inadequate for dealing with the problems of an advanced industrial society. For both Adam Smith and Ricardo there seemed to be no reason why accumulation should not go on at the maximum feasible rate —both because of the expected blessings of industrialization and the need to escape from the law of diminishing returns. Unless the needs of national defense in the modern world have in large measure recreated the classical problem, there still remains room to choose present consumption and accumulation for the future. In other words, the Classical view needs to be refined by the introduction of the concept of an optimum rate of growth.

The Marshallian economics in the hands of Pigou provided the foundations of the modern subject called Welfare Economics.[3] In line with the neo-classical tradition this subject has been mainly concerned with the efficient allocation of existing resources for consumption and production and has largely neglected the Classical question of accumulation. At a time when hedonism was already discredited in the realm of ethical philosophy, it was called upon to provide the ethical foundations of economics.

The basic assumptions of the theory were that utilities derived by individuals from the consumption of commodities were cardinally measurable, diminishing, and comparable among individuals, and that the utilities enjoyed by one individual did not depend on those enjoyed by another. On those assumptions an organization of economic resources that would yield maximum satisfaction for society could readily be prescribed.

---

[3] I shall not attempt to do justice or even to refer specifically to the wealth of literature in this field. For a comprehensive survey of the literature, see Kenneth E. Boulding's essay, "Welfare Economics," in *A Survey of Contemporary Economics*, Vol. II, ed. B. F. Haley, (1952).

The prescribed organization would be achieved in major respects under a regime of perfect competition. In fact, I know of no other way in which that organization could be achieved in an uncontrolled economy—unless our economic theory is all wrong and we cannot assume that consumers and producers follow the principles of maximizing behavior. In two major respects, however, the social optimum in the Pigouvian view would not be achieved by perfect competition. First, governmental measures might be needed to achieve the best distribution of income. For such measures, the law of diminishing marginal utility of income provided the guide and would lead to complete equality of incomes except so far as productive incentives are adversely affected. In the second place, government action might be required to abate nuisances, such as smoke, or to achieve "external economies."

The Paretian approach, followed by Hicks, Kaldor, and others, based on "indifference-curve analysis," attempted to derive welfare conclusions without recourse to the Marshallian assumptions of measurability and interpersonal comparability of utilities. As was to be expected, this approach could point to increases or decreases in welfare only in cases where everyone was better off or worse off. The rejection of interpersonal comparisons allowed no alternative, although Hicks and Kaldor have put forward the principle that welfare should be considered to have increased if everyone could be made better off by a change, whether in fact they actually were. In short, the Paretian approach necessarily provided no criterion, as did the Pigouvian, for an equitable distribution of income. Whether changes in distribution are good or bad from the viewpoint of equity must be decided by the politician or the moral philosopher—not by any techniques available to the economist.

The Paretian analysis, however, did yield the same "marginal conditions" as the Pigouvian and therefore did furnish the same support for a state of perfect competition. These marginal conditions have been stated succinctly and generally by Samuelson thus:

Necessary Marginal Conditions for an Optimum. Between any two variables, the marginal rates of substitution must be (subjectively) equal for all individuals, and (technically) equal for all alternative processes, with the common technical and subjective ratios being equivalent; otherwise there exists a physically attainable position that makes everyone better off.[4]

A further weakening of the assumptions needed to reach the marginal conditions is represented by the analysis in terms of a social welfare function. Bergson and Samuelson have shown that the assumption that one individual's utilities are independent of those enjoyed by another—as held by Pigou and Pareto—is not necessary to reach the marginal conditions. (The Bergson formulation of a social welfare function has the additional pedagogic value of making crystal-clear the fact that, as Samuelson puts it, "normative judgments depend on norms.")

A social theory cannot simply be stricken from the record. Even though intellectuals may subsequently abandon the theory, it may have won a permanent place in the social and political thinking of the society to which it relates. Welfare economics have helped to shape the attitudes of modern Western society in at least three important respects.

In the first place, the general social acceptance of governmental measures that have redistributive effects seems to me to imply that society is prepared to act as if utilities can be compared among individuals—whether or not they can be compared in some fundamental sense. While there is political disagreement about the optimum degree of progressiveness of the income tax, the principle of progressiveness itself is rarely questioned in political debate. Any economist today who proposed that public policy be based on the view that utilities are not comparable would scarcely get a political hearing. On

Comment by Paul A. Samuelson, on Boulding's essay, p. 38.

the other hand, one who asserted that definitive and final comparisons are made would have difficulty in explaining the changing social attitudes with respect to the degree of progressiveness that is generally considered fair.

A second consequence, which can be exclusively ascribed to welfare economics, is the concept of real national income and its widespread use as a measure of material well-being. On the Pigouvian or the Paretian assumptions, an increase in real national income means an increase in welfare; and in public discussion the real national income has come to be regarded as a measure of welfare. Statements such as that national income has doubled since 1929 are held to imply that national well-being has doubled. The attitude fostered by the Pigouvian welfare economics is one of crass materialism. Pigou himself states:

Changes in consumption that come about in consequence of an increase in facilities for obtaining some of the items contained in the dividend are liable to bring about changes in taste. But, when any particular kind of commodity becomes more readily available the resultant change of taste is *usually* an enhancement. Thus, when machines are sent out on trial, or articles presented in sample-packets, or pictures exhibited free to the public, the popular desire for these objects tends to be augmented. When public-houses, or lotteries, or libraries are easily accessible, the taste for drink, or gambling, or literature is not merely gratified, but is also stimulated.[5]

Most welfare economists would disagree with Pigou and would assert that welfare comparisons had no validity if changes in tastes occurred during the period under consideration. But in that event, the national income would only be a useful indicator of welfare for short periods of time. However, one eminent authority, Simon Kuznets, is prepared to grasp firmly both horns of the dilemma and assert both that the national income measure is valid and that tastes do in fact remain constant over long periods of time. Thus he asserts that:

[5] A. C. Pigou, *Economics of Welfare,* 3rd ed. (1929), pp. 84-85.

. . . We [can] compare totals over long periods, totals that include such modern gadgets as automobiles, airplanes, refrigerators, radios, etc., with those that are bare of all such items but include horse-carts, antimacassars, and petroleum used for medicinal purposes.[6]

Thus Kuznets, from a very different starting point, ends up in the same position as Pigou. Whatever the theoretical justification, which I believe to be slight, the national income has become firmly implanted in the national ideology as a measure of welfare.

As a third instance of the effect of neoclassical welfare economics on national attitudes, the support originally given to a private individualistic economy has turned very sour. At the time the welfare theories were propounded, perfect competition appeared to be an attainable goal. The subsequent theories of monopolistic competition have thoroughly dispelled that hope. Lange and Lerner have triumphantly shown that the marginal conditions have their best chance of fulfillment in a Socialist state whose objective is to enforce marginal cost pricing. By centering attention on static problems of allocation of productive resources, the welfare economists have failed to emphasize the real advantages of a market economy and have ignored the impressive dynamic performance of capitalism. Adam Smith did much better.

While the influence of welfare economics on social attitudes may have been profound, they can only be regarded as a disappointment as a guide to the policymaker—at any rate when compared with the hopes of their authors to define a social optimum. The neoclassical economists ignored the Classical problem of accumulation and growth and failed to solve the problem they posed for themselves. But they did leave one legacy that has become an indispensable part of the economist's creed—a belief in the efficiency of choice.

Every economist must believe that decisions within limited budgets reached by rational consideration of alternative

[6] Simon Kuznets, *Economic Change* (1953), pp. 204-05.

courses of action will produce more satisfactory results than those reached in other ways. If a man has a limited budget to spend on cakes and ale, he will be better satisfied if he weighs the alternatives against each other than if he arrives at a figure for cakes without considering the possibilities of ale. A mere belief in rational process of thought, without elaborate welfare hypotheses, can in this way yield the marginal conditions. Our failure to be always aware of their importance may be ascribed to the fact that our use of them in economic analysis has become almost automatic.

The Great Depression made the cure of unemployment the great social problem—to an extent that has largely faded from our minds today. Full employment emerged as a single dominating economic objective and thus assumed a role similar to that of maximum accumulation in the vision of the Classical Economists. The Keynesian analytic structure was remarkably similar to the Ricardian in its method and spirit, but naturally very different in its diagnosis and its cure. For a few years after the publication of the *General Theory,* it seemed as though policies could be approved or rejected solely by reference to their effect on aggregate demand—in the same way as a Ricardian could appeal to the effect of proposed measures on profits.

Keynes was sublimely indifferent to the preoccupation of the Neoclassicists and the Classicists with the allocation of productive resources. He simply announced his belief that the private enterprise did its job well, provided adequate employment levels were maintained—and a simple statement of faith probably carries more conviction than the tortuous reasoning of the welfare economics. I doubt that Keynes was much concerned with the distribution of income on ethical grounds: at any rate, the thrust of his theory was to make the effects on employment rather than distributive justice the main criterion. With respect to the Classical problem of growth, Keynes' position was not, "in the long run we are all dead" but "look after the short run and the long run will look after itself"—a direct reversal of the Ricardian view.

The Keynesian economics, like the Ricardian, was not destined to survive as a monolithic doctrine. As full employment was approached, the possibility, recognized in the *General Theory,* of conflict between the objectives of full employment and stability of prices became evident. The exigencies first of full mobilization and later of partial mobilization revived interest in the Classical problems as economists came to realize that economic strength depended not only on the magnitude of the national product but on its rate of increase.

III

Each of the approaches to welfare and policy that I have described was essentially a product of its time, and no one of them seems adequate as a guide to the problems of today. While economic growth may demand major attention, distributive questions have by no means disappeared from the public consciousness. Though there may be good reason to believe that a recurrence of the depression of the thirties is unlikely, governments have recognized a responsibility for the stability of employment that was unheard of a generation ago. Finally, the requirements of national defense seem likely to mean indefinite postponement of an economy of abundance; and the neoclassical problem of economic efficiency will continue to be pertinent.

The economist must attempt to formulate a compromise among various, and possibly conflicting, economic objectives. He must attempt to discuss the economic objectives of society, to remove contradictions among them, and to harmonize economic objectives with those that lie outside the economic field. To revert to my medical analogy, he should diagnose and prescribe for the economic health of society. In doing so, he must recognize that society is in a process of growth and change and that an optimum in the static sense has little meaning or significance. Economic health cannot be appraised by economic criteria alone but only in relation to political and social health. The economist, like the medical doctor, has a more active and positive role when things are going badly than when they are going well.

I suggest that, leaving aside its international policy, the economic policy of an advanced industrial economy, particularly that of the United States, should achieve a compromise among these objectives:

1. Continued economic growth
2. High and stable employment
3. Reasonable stability of the price level
4. Equitable distribution of income and social security
5. Allocation of resources through the market mechanism
6. Conservation of cultural and material resources.

In the space at my disposal I can do no more than indicate, by some brief notes, the importance of these objectives and the possibilities of conflict or compatibility among them.

1. By continued economic growth I mean continued increase of real per-capita income. Although the intellectual foundations of the national income concept may be weak, we have learned to live with the concept and to attach significance to variations in its behavior. If national income increases from year to year at a certain rate, that epitomizes for the interpreter of the figures a combination of increased living standards in terms of calories, vitamins, housing space, etc.; the appearance of a stream of new products on the market; and a corresponding obsolescence of old products. These factors produce the sensation of improvement and change that we regard as increased material well-being.

Although objective measurements of welfare may be ill-founded, there can be no doubt that everyone thinks he knows when he is better off in a material sense—even though his illusions may be shattered later on; and after acute deficiencies in living standards have been removed, the sensation of change and improvement rather than the level of consumption may well be the dominant factor in the individual's sense of well-being.

A general sense of improvement is, I believe, a necessary condition for political and social stability—and incidentally for the preservation of the American economic way of life. Were it not for the prospects that exist in this country of economic improvement for all classes, political pressure for redistribution would be intensified and might in time react adversely on the rate of growth. The stationary state of the Classical Economists, whether the dismal one of Ricardo or the beneficent one of John Stuart Mill, seems to be utterly incompatible with our political and economic institutions. On the other hand, the rate of growth can be too rapid from the point of view of social stability. The process of "creative destruction"—the emergence of new products, the extinction of obsolete occupations, transfers of the labor force among regions, the emergence of new wealth and the liquidation of old—all tend to generate social tensions that react against the sense of greater well-being. We need what the Classical Economists failed to provide, the concept of an optimum rate of growth or change.

In the modern world, the needs of national security alone demand a continually growing economy. Experience has shown that consumption standards can be curtailed only with the utmost difficulty to release the resources needed in times of mobilization. In fact, consumption standards for large sections of the labor force may have to be raised to provide production incentives. The capacity to increase total production is indispensable if defense emergencies are to be adequately met, and that capacity only exists in a changing and growing economy.

In normal times, other than defense emergencies, the

attainment of a given rate of growth requires an appropriate relation between the increase in income saved and invested and the increase devoted to raising consumption standards. The ability and the desire to increase consumption, as the classic Brookings studies emphasized, is essential. Many, if not most, of the possibilities of profitable investment occur in the production of goods mass-produced for mass consumption. These possibilities will therefore not be realized unless increases in mass purchasing power accompany increases in income. On the other hand, the supply of saving must be adequate to make room for the investment required to achieve the desired rate of growth. With adequate knowledge of the structure of the economy obtained through input-output analysis and the analysis of capital requirements, these saving and consumption conditions can conceivably be given empirical content.

The question to which we may never know the answer concerns the conditions required to evoke entrepreneurial endeavor. Are those economists right who assert that entrepreneurship is a tender plant that flourishes only in an atmosphere of economic and social privilege, or those who urge that nothing matters but a high level of demand and a labor shortage, or those who argue that the functions of entrepreneurship have been bureaucratized and employees of corporations need be accorded privileges of the same order as those accorded to other bureaucrats? To these questions we have no conclusive answers and possibly never will. The record of the past is inconclusive; direct inquiry yields biased answers; an experimentation is not permitted. Policy decisions must inevitably be taken on the basis of highly uncertain evidence. Since anticapitalist measures are unlikely to be reversed, I suggest that they should be undertaken, if at all, with considerable caution.

2. The importance of high and stable employment as an

objective of policy can now almost be regarded as self-evident. To judge by political attitudes at the present time (1954), any political party would face defeat if it permitted unemployment to reach 10 per cent of the labor force. The interesting subject for discussion is whether there is likely to be conflict or compatibility between this and other objectives of policy, particularly continued economic growth. But here again we enter the realm of difficult and unanswered questions.

Does a labor shortage or an "industrial reserve army" create conditions more favorable to economic growth? The labor shortage produces an incentive to substitute capital for labor. Indeed, substitution may be necessary for survival. On the other hand, the reserve army, if it is not too large, symbolizes an atmosphere traditionally considered "favorable to business." Although final judgment is not yet, and may never be, possible, the experience of the past decade gives considerable support to the labor shortage side of the argument.

Full employment and labor shortage, however, are likely to involve wage-price inflationary pressure—if carried far enough. Under modern conditions such pressures are more likely to be suppressed by direct controls than to be allowed to dissipate themselves in price increases. Even without empirical evidence, I am prepared to rely on economic reasoning to conclude that widespread use of direct price and wage controls is inimical to growth. No one has ever devised a system of controls that does not relate legal prices and wages to the price and wage structure that prevailed in some base period. While the nexus with the base period rarely amounts to a "freeze," if it is broken entirely, the control system has virtually evaporated. Consequently, in a changing and growing economy, legal prices and wages are necessarily unadapted to the current economic situation. And the industries that are most likely to be prejudiced are those that are growing most rapidly and are embarking on new lines of economic endeavor. In short, control systems, in practice, are prejudicial to the process of growth and change.

Serious conflict between the high employment objective and that of economic growth may arise from the means employed. There need be no incompatibility—if, for instance, measures to increase employment consist of tax reductions, appropriately distributed among taxes on consumption and taxes on enterprise, and interest-rate reductions. But ideological or supersititious objections to such policies, frequently raised by pro-business interests themselves, may lead governments to pursue the objective of high employment by policies that are inimical to economic growth.

3. Arguments concerning the desirable behavior of the price level seem to have narrowed down to those favoring stability and those in support of a gradually rising price level. Modern price rigidities and the recognition that relative wage adjustments must be achieved through differential increases seem to have excluded a falling general price level as a feasible policy objective. Price stability means that the best that fixed money incomes can do is to hold their own; they do not participate in general productivity increases. A steadily rising price level means continued erosion of the real value of fixed incomes.

From the point of view of growth and employment, the weight of the argument appears to be on the side of a rising price (and wage) level—essentially because it does afford business and governments continued relief from "deadweight" fixed money commitments. Arguments that rising prices inevitably degenerate into serious inflation do not appear tenable, provided uncertainty remains with respect to short-run price movements.

Even though a rising price level may be more favorable to economic performance, there appears to be no reason to exclude price stability as a policy objective if it is desired for other reasons. The arguments for a stable price level rest on political and social grounds. There can be little doubt that preservation of the real value of rentier incomes, whether institutional or individual, does in itself contribute to political and social stability. Whether one favors a stable price level depends on one's political preferences—and not on economic analysis. As an employee of a privately endowed institution, I confess to a certain amount of bias in the matter.

4. That the distribution of income among individuals cannot be left to look after itself can now be regarded as a political axiom—due, I believe, in considerable measure to the influence of the utilitarian economics. Here again the major question that calls for discussion is whether or not prevailing notions of equity contribute to or conflict with other economic objectives.

The consequences of conflict can be serious, even from the point of view of equality. As has been pointed out by Schumpeter and others, the greatest equalizer from the real income standpoint is capitalistic development itself. The difference between a Cadillac and a Ford is far less than the difference between a Ford and a bicycle. The preoccupation of politicians and statisticians with money incomes obscures this essential fact. There can be little doubt that redistributive measures, if carried far enough, can impair the prospects of economic growth and have actually done so in some countries.

On the other hand, redistributive measures may be needed to facilitate the process of growth. There is no reason to believe that the pricing mechanism alone will necessarily generate the mass-consumption demand for the products of mass production. If the forces of competition are not strong enough to ensure the profit margins that will ensure expansion, public policy may require either governmental intervention in the pricing policy of business or fiscal measures to redistribute incomes.

5. As we saw above, the neoclassical welfare economics may have done more to discredit the market mechanism than to justify it. The prescribed ideal is so far from reality that the welfare arguments seem to support governmental controls rather than the operation of the market. But the advocates of controls usually avoid the crucial question whether the controllers will be greatly interested in the economists' welfare criteria. Experience with controlled systems seems to indicate the controllers have criteria of their own. The choice seems to lie between allocation according to the arbitrary whims of authority or allocation according to the anonymous processes of the market. There is strong reason for preferring the latter method both because it is anonymous and because it works smoothly. Simply to avoid the irritations of controls is an objective of major importance.

The most decisive argument for the market mechanism, however, may be political rather than economic. A complicated control system necessarily means increased bureaucratic control. Legislatures can do little more than lay down the most general principles for the administration of controls, and cannot effectively review what has been done. Long continued use of controls must be considered inconsistent with political democracy.

6. The final objective of policy relates to the conservation of values that would otherwise disappear in the process of creative destruction. What, for instance, should be done to support regions of the country that are losing out in the economic race? Should they be depopulated in the name of "progress" or should "progress" be retarded in order to support them? In my opinion, a country as rich as the United States can and should abate the rigor of the ruthless application of economic law.

Public measures should also be considered to preserve cultural values. The educational system today is suffering as much from the consequences of industrialization as from inflation. When productivity increases in manufacture, the typical family appears to devote a larger part of its income to the products of industry that have become relatively cheap and a smaller part to education, which has become relatively expensive. The alternatives in education may be mechanization or subsidization. The television screen can displace the individual teacher or the teaching profession can be made attractive through the provision of (federal) government subsidies. Similar questions arise with respect to the theater and music. Is it socially desirable that the legitimate stage or the concert should become increasingly the privilege of the well-to-do? But perhaps in those cases the trend to mechanization for the masses of the population has gone too far to be reversed or controlled.

The economist concerned with the general direction of policy must, I submit, consider all these objectives of policy and possibly others that I have not listed. He cannot and should not attempt to chart a definite course of action for government; he should rather attempt to define limits for political debate and point to implications of political action—particularly long-run implications—that are not visible to the naked political eye. If these tasks seem vague and unsatisfactory to many economists, the foregoing discussion has indicated many areas where there is urgent need for analysis unadulterated with policy.

One final point: many discussions of economic policy, possibly including this one, tend to create the impression that the economy is always ready to veer widely off its course and only the skill and the sagacity of government can hope to maintain its direction. The events of the last decade should dispel this impression. The normal process of growth has continued, and extraordinary stability of employment has been maintained, despite the vicissitudes of demobilization, postwar reconstruction, partial mobilization, and partial demobilization. These results must be ascribed more to the inherent forces of stability and growth than to the wisdom of economic policy. It may be enough for government action to move generally in the right direction rather than to follow a carefully calculated plan of action. In that event, the task of framing economic policy comes well within the limits of human capacity.

2

From Theory to Public Policy[1]

JOSEPH J. SPENGLER[2]

It should be permissible to consider from an exclusively theoretical standpoint, a subject of general interest which has so many different sides.

A. A. Cournot

The problem is to be solved . . . by connecting the phenomenon to be accounted for with the ultimate principles of the science to which it belongs.

J. E. Cairnes

MY PRIMARY CONCERN in this lecture is the contribution that theory may make to public policy. After defining theory and delimiting the area of public policy and its objectives, I shall show how theory has contributed, or may contribute, to the formation of public policy and to the specification and assessment of policy objectives. Finally, I shall touch upon the limitations to which the use of theory is presently subject and indicate certain implications of these limitations.

I

The term theory as used in this paper embraces whatever apparatus of thought may be effectively employed to explore particular areas of reality including that of values and value orientations. For our purposes, it may usually be thought of as including the various models that may be utilized to represent the way or ways in which relevant variable elements in

---

[1] I am indebted to R. T. Cole and C. B. Hoover for critical comments and suggestions.
[2] Professor of Economics, Duke University.

23

human behavior supposedly interact with one another, together with the extent to which this interaction is conditioned
by circumstances that are fixed or likely to remain comparatively constant for a sufficiently long time. Since, however,
the variable elements in human behavior are but modes of
the behavior of individuals, acting either as individuals or
as agents of collective bodies (e.g., a corporation, a foundation, a family, a parish church), it may be more meaningful
for the present discussion to think of our models as repre-
senting the ways in which individuals supposedly interact with
respect to more or less explicitly defined objectives and
subject to more or less carefully specified restraints.

While initially our models may be described with varying
degrees of specificity, they must, if they are to be used with
respect to policy formation, which is an empirical matter,
be described with a minimal necessary degree of specificity
and given a sufficient amount of empirical content. For
example, one might say, in terms of a Marshallian demand
model, that if Country A reduced its export prices, the rest
of the world would purchase a greater quantity of Country
A's exports, or that if the rest of the world raised its export
prices, Country A would purchase a smaller quantity of these
higher-priced exports. But one could not build a trade
policy on so general and unspecific a model. Thus, if Country
A is considering devaluing its currency in the hope of elimi-
nating an excess of payments for imports over receipts for
exports, it must, before it acts, determine whether its demand
for imports and the demand of the rest-of-the-world for its
(i.e., A's) exports are sufficiently elastic individually and in
combination to produce the result intended.[3]

Concerning the general meaning of the term public policy
there is little dispute. The Oxford Dictionary definition constitutes an adequate point of departure: "A course of action

---

[3] See A. O. Hirschman, "Devaluation and the Trade Balance: A Note,"
Review of Economics and Statistics, XXXI (1949), 50-53.

adopted and pursued by a government, party, ruler, statesman, etc.; any given course of action adopted as advantageous or expedient." For this conception of policy, of which examples are reported at least as far back as the fifteenth century, probably came into being during the period when the national state was developing and men were becoming enamored of the view that the apparatus of state could be employed in times of peace even as in times of war to realize, or to make more likely of realization, avowed objectives with which, as a rule, the not too well-defined welfare of the commonwealth was associated. The origins of this conception presumably are of even greater antiquity, since governments usually have pursued objectives and since the term policy itself stems etymologically from classic Greek concepts. Nonetheless, a better savor of the modern meaning is to be had from the writings of men like Petty and Steuart than from those of Plato and Cicero. For Petty attributed in part to differences in the "policy of the places" the relatively greater economic progress found in Holland than in France,[4] while Steuart declared himself to be setting down "principles of policy" for the guidance of the "statesman."[5] This meaning was retained by Adam Smith and the classical economists, together with their liberal associates, even though many of them favored restricting the role of the state to "the establishment and the enforcement of law;"[6] and some even subscribed to Lord Macaulay's dictum apropos the interventionism of Frederick the Great, that "to be ruled by a busybody is more than human nature can bear."[7] This meaning continues to be

[4] William Petty, *Political Arithmetick* (London, 1690) Chap. 1, esp. pp. 10, 21 ff. C. H. Hull, *The Economic Writings of Sir William Petty* (Cambridge, 1899), pp. 255, 261 ff.

[5] Sir James Steuart, *An Inquiry into the Principles of Political Economy; Being An Essay on the Science of Domestic Policy in Free Nations* (1767), Preface. See also Adam Smith, *The Wealth of Nations* (1776), Bk. IV.

[6] See Lionel Robbins, *The Theory of Economic Policy in English Classical Political Economy* (1952), p. 193.

[7] "Frederick the Great," *The Works of Lord Macaulay*, ed. Lady Treveleyan, VI (1866), 673.

accepted by contemporary social scientists, some of whom would give even more employment to the apparatus of state than their mercantilist forbears recommended.

II

The dictionary and related meanings with which the term public policy has been clothed are not sufficiently specific for most purposes of analysis, since analysis usually has to do with particular, concrete, empirical situations. In ordinary discourse, the term commonly refers either to what we shall call policy objectives, or to both such an objective and the institutional instruments designed for its realization. It is essential, however, that the content of a policy be distinguished from the content of the avowed purpose of such policy. Should the actual outcome of a policy differ from its intended outcome, the content of the actual outcome must be distinguished both from the content of the intended outcome and from the content of the policy itself. It is essential also that the administration of policy be distinguished sharply from its content, since the manner in which a policy is administered conditions the results that are consequent upon the pursuit of such policy.

It would appear that a policy is best defined in terms of what it does, or in terms of the operations composing it. Such definition of a policy may or may not be virtually equivalent to one expressed in terms of the set of rules and practices established by responsible authorities for the accomplishment of a given policy objective. If, as the result of trial and error, legislative modification, judicial decision, and administrative experience, the established rules and practices become sufficiently precise and sufficiently numerous, the content of a particular policy, defined in terms of the operations composing it, will correspond closely to its content as defined by relevant rules and practices. If, on the contrary, only a relatively small number of explicit, formal rules have been established, the content of a policy can be but imperfectly suggested thereby; it is necessary then to turn also to the operations composing the policy, operations that may include, along with other matter, formal and informal arrangements for carrying out the rules in question. To illustrate: the late Henry Simons proposed that the objectives of monetary policy be sought through the establishment of a suitable set of rules with which individuals and organizations would be required to comply; more recently, Friedman recommended that the maintenance of economic stability be attained through compliance with a stipulated set of monetary and fiscal principles. From the rules laid down in each of these proposals, one could get a notion of the content of the policy implied; but that notion would be incomplete. One would have to examine the operations employed to carry out the stipulated rules in order to discover fully the content and meaning of the policy in question; and these operations would not all have come into being until the relevant exigencies of the situation had been taken into account.[8]

While it is essential to distinguish between a policy and the organization that is responsible for administering this policy, it is somewhat easier to make this distinction analytically than to make it empirically. For the content of an administrative organization tends in some measure to pervade the content of the policy that organization is charged to carry out. Some of the practices established within the framework of an administrative organization may form a part of the content of policy as we have defined it. Again, some members of the staff of an administrative organization may enjoy discretion, the manner of exercise of which

[8] See Henry Simons, *Economic Policy for a Free Society* (1948), pp. 160 ff. and *passim;* Milton Friedman, "A Monetary and Fiscal Framework for Economic Stability," *American Economic Review,* XXXVIII (1948), 245 ff. Simons' paper was first published in 1936. See also on adaptation to exigencies, Talcott Parsons, *The Social System* (1951), pp. 168-69, 184 ff.

conditions the content of the policies carried out by that organization. And so on. Despite this tendency for the content of policy and the content of administration empirically to overlap, it is possible to keep policy and organization conceptually distinct. It is important that this be so because, within limits, the extent to which the purpose of a policy is realizable turns on the skill with which it is administered.

Before we examine in detail the distinction between policy and objective of policy, two points should be noted. First, policies may be classified, as Bertrand Russell has classified "causal laws," into "those concerned with persistence and those concerned with change."[9] For we may conceive of a policy as consisting of a set of operations with which there is associated either realization of an objective that remains free of growth and novelty, or that of an objective into which growth and novelty enter as time passes. In the former instance the resulting objective situation would be analogous to Schumpeter's representation of "the circular flow of economic life" as unchanging;[10] in the latter instance the objective outcome would be analogous to a "flow of economic life" undergoing change in a relatively orderly (disorderly) manner. Second, even though a policy is well conceived and executed, the objective it is designed to bring about is likely to be realized only imperfectly; for concrete outcomes reflect, besides the combined influence of policy intent and policy administration, the impact of events beyond the control of the policy formulators and administrators.

The content of the objective of a policy needs to be distinguished from the content of the policy itself. This distinction is easier to make conceptually than empirically. Analytically, one may conceive of a policy and its objective as

[9] Bertrand Russell, *Human Knowledge: Its Scope and Limits* (1948), p. 310.

[10] J. A. Schumpeter, *The Theory of Economic Development* (1934), Chap. 1.

being adjoining links in a means-end chain of links connecting action with ultimate goals or ends. A policy is always instrumental in character, while the goal of policy, though usually also largely instrumental in character, is at least a step less removed than policy from the ultimate goal and hence a kind of end. At the empirical level, by contrast, the distinction between means and end is less clear. For goal values are not always easy to distinguish from instrumental values; and the instrumental values sometimes have reflected back into themselves some of the value associated with the ends of these instrumental values, or are otherwise interpenetrated by noninstrumental value.[11] In practice, of course, the ease with which policy and policy objectives are distinguishable at the empirical level varies greatly. Thus policies and policy objectives relating to the balance of payments[12] are nicely separable, while policy and policy objectives under the Sherman Act, or under housing legislation, appear somewhat intertwined.

When a policy and its objectives are so defined as to make the one distinguishable from the other, it is possible to determine with precision whether the actual outcome of a policy corresponds closely to the intended outcome. Furthermore, when both policy and policy objective are readily distinguishable, it may be possible to determine with precision whether a given objective is more likely to be realized, or to be realized with relatively greater efficiency and/or economy (it being given that acceptable criteria of efficiency or economy are applicable), through the pursuit of a given policy than some alternative.

[11] See *Toward a General Theory of Action*, ed. Talcott Parsons and E. A. Shils (1951), pp. 412-13 and *passim*; Talcott Parsons, *The Structure of Social Action* (1937), *passim*; H. A. Simon, *Administrative Behavior* (1945), pp. 59, 62 ff., 184 ff.

[12] See J. E. Meade, *The Theory of International Economic Policy*, Vol. I, *The Balance of Payments* (1951).

III

Up to now I have implicitly evaded a question that should be faced. I have defined a policy in terms of its operations and assigned it a lower order in the means-end hierarchy than the objective that this policy is intended to realize. In so doing I have run counter, I believe, to what many would consider a superior approach. For they would employ the term policy to represent what I have called the objective of policy, and they would look upon that which I have called policy as but the means or instrument selected to realize policy.

Objections to this approach have already been suggested. Most basic of these objections is the fact that very rarely can one infer from something like a new piece of legislation what it means with any degree of specificity, let alone what objective it was intended to bring about. Consider, for example, the Sherman Antitrust Act. The evidence is very clear that long before this act became law in 1890 a strong antimonopoly tradition prevailed in the United States. The act itself, having been enacted at a time when men's awareness of the presence of monopolistic combinations was increasing even more rapidly than the growth of these combinations in number and power, was directed against arrangements that operated to restrain, or were designed to restrain, commerce "among the several States, or with foreign nations." But the terms of prohibition were left vague, perhaps with intent, and it became necessary for the courts to give specific meaning and content to the statute.

One could not infer with much precision from this statute, even as interpreted from time to time by the courts and as supplemented by other statutes similarly interpreted, what was the policy of the United States in respect of the mainte-nance of "competition" in interstate commerce. I have in mind not so much the fact, important though it be, that the

majority opinion of the courts has undergone change, to say
nothing of minority opinion, which as recently as 1911 included an approval of monopoly pricing,[13] I have in mind
rather that at any time there is an avowed objective (or perhaps more accurately, divers avowed objectives) of the
Sherman Act and there is an actual outcome, which may be
defined in terms of decisions rendered, actions taken, etc.;
but neither is definable with precision and completeness, and
rarely is an avowed objective equivalent to the actual outcome.
If we turn to what the Federal Trade Commission and the
Department of Justice are doing, to judicial, administrative,
and related statements of what is permissible, prohibited, or
doubtful, and to sufficiently accurate estimates of the manner
in which parties subject to the Sherman Act are responding
to it, we get a definition of policy that is empirical, opera-
tional, and relatively complete.

It is true that frequently the content of policy, thus defined, overlaps in considerable degree the content of the
realized (if not necessarily the intended) outcome of policy.
But there is a difference. The content of a policy, as we have
defined it, stands in a different context than does the content
of the actual outcome, or that of the avowed objective of this
policy. The content of the former stands in an essentially
factual and descriptive context. The content of the outcome
of a policy, and even more, the content of the objective of
a policy, stands in a context that is permeated with value,
if for no other reason than that its position in the means-end
chain is closer to the pole about which ultimate goals and
values cluster. Accordingly, that content which is common
to both policy and outcome of policy has a somewhat different
meaning when examined in the context of policy than when
examined in the context of outcome of policy.

Ultimately, I suppose, I am arguing that policy should be

[13] See the dissenting opinion of Mr. Justice Holmes in *Dr. Miles Medical
Co.* v. *John D. Park & Sons Co.*, 220 U. S. 373 (1911).

defined, in so far as possible, in factual rather than in valuational terms; and that making the term refer to operations renders it more factual and less valuational than it would be if it referred instead to supposed outcomes or avowed objectives of these operations. This line of argument implies further that whatever is not reducible to terms of empirical operations should be treated as the objective of policy even though its position in the means-end chain falls short of what is considered the ultimate value pole.

This line of argument is not intended to depreciate the importance of policy objectives, but to recognize that it is much easier to treat of policy than of policy objectives in concrete, factual terms. It is not intended to suggest that theory has little to contribute to the formulation, clarification, and assessment of policy objectives. For economic and sociological theory, when bearing upon policy objectives, includes, as does political theory, what Sabine calls "an estimate of probabilities and an estimate of values."[14] We shall touch upon this later.

IV

Let us turn now to the contribution that theory has made, or may make, to the formulation and implementation of policy, reserving until later, consideration of the office of theory in respect of policy objectives. For the sake of expositive convenience, our discussion will be concentrated upon the replacement of old by new policies.

A change in policy comes about in a society when an old objective gives way to a new objective, or when a given objective is no longer believed realizable in adequate measure through pursuit of a policy theretofore deemed sufficient. Dissatisfaction at the supposed lack of correspondence be-

[14] G. H. Sabine, "What Is a Political Theory?" *Journal of Politics,* I (1939), 5. See also D. H. Robertson, "On Sticking to One's Last," *Economic Journal,* LIX (1949), 508-09; A. B. Wolfe, "Economy and Democracy," *American Economic Review,* XXXIV (1944), 1-20.

tween policy and policy objective must be felt by individuals with enough political power in the aggregate to produce changes in legislation intended to make the desired policy objective realizable. We shall couch our argument in terms of legislation on the postulate, which may not always be valid, that changes in administrative decrees are not capable of producing a sufficient change in policy. The number re- —quired to be animated by this belief depends, *ceteris paribus,* upon the comparative proportions of the population who oppose, are indifferent to, or are disposed to acquiesce in, the changes in question. The particular changes that are brought about, given that the change favorers prevail, will depend upon many things, some transient and some relatively permanent, some objective and some subjective in character, and so on. Among these determining factors should be included the state of relevant socio-economic theory, the extent to which use is made of this body of theory, and the capacity, itself partly dependent upon the state of theory, of a society to innovate various policies (or institutional arrangements) suited to realize some (not usually very precise) policy objective.

We may turn to agriculture for examples of the coming into being of what some considered a lack of correspondence between policy and policy objective. This happened in Europe when, after the close of the American Civil War and the extension of rail systems into wheat-growing states, cereal began to flow into Europe at declining prices, with the result that many European states had to modify what had been their agricultural policies. Their responses varied. Both industrially expanding Germany and demographically stationary France resorted to strong agricultural protectionism, while Italy fell back upon a weaker form of agricultural protectionism, supplemented by external emigration. Holland and Denmark continued to allow wheat to move in tariff-free but modified their agriculture, the Danes in particular ending up by reorienting their agriculture to intensive animal husbandry. Britain continued the free trade policy established upon the repeal of the Corn Laws, to the partial dissolution of the political strength of her agricultural interest. In the generation of these decisions, theory seems not to have played an important role. In Britain contemporary economic theory may have strengthened the hands of those favoring free trade; while in Germany a false theory, to the effect that industrial-export and agricultural-import markets would eventually be denied her, gave support to agricultural protectionism and to programs for the prevention of the industrialization of potentially competitor countries. In all six of these countries the final verdict was shaped by a variety of factors, among them the values regnant in each of the societies and the state of intergroup relations.[15]

Theory might of course have made a greater contribution than it did. It might have shown that, under the circumstances, the free trade solution was best, particularly if accompanied by reimbursement of those who would be adversely affected in the short-run by the inflow of tariff-free cereal grains. In the event that this solution had not been completely acceptable (and I am ruling out, for the present, such qualifications as might be suggested by modern welfare-economic theory) and that need for a compromise of dissimilar interests had been indicated, sociological theory might have disclosed the range of interest overlap within which a solution, that did not fall short of the minimal requirements of any affected party, was to be found.[16] Whether, given this

---

[15] This paragraph is based largely upon C. P. Kindleberger, "Group Behavior and International Trade," *Journal of Political Economy*, LIX (1951), 30-46. Concerning the role played by invalid economic theory in Germany, see A. O. Hirschman, *National Power and the Structure of Foreign Trade* (1945), pp. 146-51.

[16] On the area within which authoritative agreement is to be found see C. I. Bernard, *The Functions of the Executive* (1938), Chap. 12, and H. A. Simon, "A Formal Theory of the Employment Relationship," *Econometrica*, XIX (1951), 293 ff. A similar point of view pervades

information, a "better" point of "agreement" than was arrived at in the area of overlap, would have been chosen, is not absolutely clear. It seems probable, however, that this area might have been relocated and a "better" point selected, had the attainable findings of both economic and sociological theory been taken into account; and it seems certain that today, given a similar confrontation, a better solution could and probably would be had if economic and sociological theory were employed to locate the area within which acceptable solutions lie and to indicate the probable empirical implications of alternative solutions.

Turning to America, we encounter a somewhat different course of events. The "surplus" problem first began to receive considerable attention after World War I when expression was given to the idea of price parity and to proposals for reserving to the farmer a protected, domestic produce market in which relatively high prices would prevail. Because of presidential opposition, nothing came of this for some years except a program for supporting certain prices through governmental purchases. After 1932, however, Congress approved a set of backward-facing institutional arrangements designed to support farm prices and incomes and to ease risk burdens that supposedly bore relatively heavily upon agriculturalists.[17]

While economic theory, now more advanced than after the Civil War when European countries first faced a "surplus" problem, was employed in the construction of these protectionist arrangements, it was not used by the architects of these arrangements to appraise their impact in welfare

J. R. Commons' discussions of bargaining, negotiation, etc., in his *Institutional Economics* (1936).

[17] For a historical review see M. R. Benedict, *Farm Policies of the United States* (1953); and, on the importance of the empirical content of agricultural models, Carl Kaysen and J. H. Lorie, "A Note on Professor Schultz's Analysis of the Long Run Agricultural Problem," *Review of Economics and Statistics*, XXX (1948), 286 ff.

terms, nor was sociological theory used to ascertain whether
the nonfarm elements in the population considered these
arrangements consonant with their own interests and welfare
conceptions. It was not even recognized that, on the Ricardian
principles that undermined the rationale of the English
Corn Laws, the new arrangements stood to benefit markedly
only those who owned land at the time the new arrangements
went into effect. It is possible, of course, that had employment theory been well developed in 1933, the Roosevelt
administration would not have had recourse to such an
amalgam of heterogeneous antidepression measures—among
them, the new program for agriculture—as it sought to put
into effect in and after 1933. As it was, however, three circumstances contributed greatly to the introduction of agricultural protectionism: the depression climate of opinion; the
fact (usually present when legislation favoring special interests is enacted) that the gains were concentrated in the hands
of a minority while the costs were dispersed over the whole
population; and the disproportionately great political power
enjoyed by representatives of those elements in the population
who believed themselves especially dependent upon agriculture for a livelihood.

Despite the fact that emotionalism has pervaded some
recent discussions of monetary policy, the formulation of
monetary and foreign-exchange policies usually has been
shaped in very large measure by economic theory.[18] This is
apparent, for example, in the discussions of policy alternatives
that took place during and after the Napoleonic Wars, World
War I, and World War II. The content of theory changed
in the interval, passing from the simpler quantitative ap-

[18] E.g., see the summary accounts in S. E. Harris, et al., "The Controversy Over Monetary Policy," *Review of Economics and Statistics*, XXXIII
(1951), 179-200; James Tobin, "Monetary Policy and the Management of
the Public Debt: The Patman Inquiry," *ibid.*, XXXV (1953), 118-27.
Cf. also E. A. Goldenweiser, *Monetary Management* (1949), *passim*, on
aspects of policy and decision-making.

proaches of Ricardo's day to the complex notions of clearings, spending sensitivity, interest impact, etc., encountered in the 1940's. But policy tended to reflect the theory of the day, at least so long as the objective of policy was suitably defined.[19]

Several factors appear to be responsible for this relatively great (or so it seems) contribution of theory to policy formation respecting matters of money and foreign exchange. At each important conjuncture in the past, economists appear to have been in substantial agreement concerning the content and implications of monetary and exchange theory. Moreover, policy was formed by a skillful minority largely free of what Henry Taylor called "the forced familiarities of the hustings."[20] Furthermore, although the interest groups composing society were never wholly agreed respecting policy objectives, almost none pressed for a great departure from price stability, and almost all favored a policy that gave promise of persisting with relatively little change. Whether the contribution of theory could still be so great if, as may well happen, the maintenance of full employment entailed continually rising prices, remains to be seen. It would appear, however, that then policy and policy objective respecting money and foreign exchange would be greatly influenced, as have agricultural policy and policy objectives, by the distribution of political power.[21]

I should remark parenthetically that were I to define monetary and exchange theory more broadly and include thereunder

[19] Clark Warburton has traced difficulties with our monetary system to "the absence of a suitably defined objective for the guidance of central bank operations and an adequate economic information and analysis service." See his "Rules and Implements for Monetary Policy," *Journal of Finance,* VIII (1953), 1 ff., and "Monetary Difficulties and the Structure of the Monetary System," *ibid.,* VII (1952), 523-45.

[20] *The Statesman,* Reprint Series 2, p. 174.

[21] See M. W. Reder's analysis in "The General Level of Money Wages," *Proceedings of the Third Annual Meeting, Industrial Relations Research Association* (1950), pp. 1-17.

questions of investment and repressed inflation, history would reveal more conflict than I have reported. Consider, for example, the German and similar post-1945 monetary situations. Then some economists advocated (correctly, I would say) removing the "excess" of money from the economy, whilst others preferred using controls to prevent the "excess" from pressing prices upward. Even in these situations, however, the policy objectives were quite similar. Dispute arose over policy, because the disputants disagreed respecting the response of individuals and economies to continuation of a variety of controls.

It has been indicated that theory can contribute effectively to the formation of policy only if other circumstances are such as to permit its use. Sometimes the interval during which other circumstances are favorable is quite short. A case in point is the Schuman Plan. Economic and political theory apparently contributed appreciably to the innovation of this plan. The plan did not, however, meet with the desires of most of the interest groups that it would affect. Yet the plan was adopted. For these interests were outmaneuvered by the sponsors of the plan in that short postwar period during which international sources of power greatly outweighed national sources; and there was brought into legal and institutional being the whole apparatus of the Schuman Plan. Had the sponsors not proceeded with so much skill and speed, it is improbable that the plan would have been adopted.[22] Most likely the sponsors were gifted with Cavour's *tact de choses possibles*. It is conceivable, however, that sociological theory would have disclosed a need to translate the plan speedily into international and national law.

Having reviewed somewhat discursively past experience

---

[22] See Horst Mendershausen, "First Tests of the Schuman Plan," *Review of Economics and Statistics,* XXXV (1953), 270-71; Raymond Aron, "Problem of European Integration," *Lloyds Bank Review* (April 1953), pp. 1-17.

with policy formation, let us summarize briefly how theory may contribute to the formulation of policy, it being taken for granted that such formulation will always be conditioned by the state of theory. First, at the time when a policy change seems indicated, theory may be employed to discover and interpret facts having to do with whether a policy change is really indicated, with the comparatively careful definition of policy objectives, with the implications of these objectives, and with the disclosure of the main policy alternatives available. Second, upon information conerning these policies having been made available, theory may contribute to the discovery and assessment of acts having to do with which, if any, of the policy alternatives is preferable on technical grounds, with the isolation of the area of overlap (or acceptance) within which the chosen solution must lie, and with the implications of various solutions found in this area. Third, theory may then be employed to assist in the construction of an effective organization suited to carry out the preferred policy. Finally, theory may be employed to help assess the effectiveness with which the preferred policy is being administered and to discover whether, in fact, the selected policy is accomplishing its intended purpose.

V

The capacity of theory to contribute to the formation of policy is subject to various limitations. First, policy that appears feasible on certain hypotheses may actually be unfeasible because the hypotheses in question are not currently in sufficient keeping with underlying reality. To illustrate: A. P. Lerner has proposed that governments employ "counterspeculation" against certain monopolists and monopsonists, thereby making perfectly elastic both the demand curves confronting the monopolists and the supply curves confronting the monopsonists. But as Machlup (among others) has correctly pointed out, "the practical, political and administrative difficulties of operating the device of 'counterspeculation' would be overwhelming and might cause a waste of resources greater than that involved in the monopolistic restriction of production." Even so, this type of argument, a common resort of what Toynbee calls the dominant minority, must be employed judiciously, since otherwise its use may retard progress. For, as Robertson has remarked, what if this type of argument had silenced those who saw in deficit-financing a remedy for trade depression; and what if it were to silence those who find in wage reductions and the removal of subsidies a possible cure for a persisting adverse balance of payments.[23]

Second, the capacity of theory to contribute to policy formulation is limited by the multiplicity of policy combinations from among which choice must be made, and by the almost inevitable disposition of the theorist, especially when confronted by such multiplicity or by very complex situations, to indulge in oversimplification at the theoretical level. Meade, in his discussion of balance-of-payments policy, comes up in one place with 25 policy combinations and in another with nearly 29 billion policy-plus-policy-objective combinations. It being hard, under such conditions, to choose a policy, even in the absence of social and political constraints, the theorist tends to simplify his analysis and throw out many of the combinations. In so doing, however, he may depart too widely from reality and thus accentuate difficulties already occasioned by his inability to fill his models with sufficiently specific empirical content. There is much to be said, therefore, in support of generalizing H. G. Johnson's conclusion that "economic theory" can "most usefully" be applied "to problems of economic policy . . . within the con-

[23] A. P. Lerner, *The Economics of Control* (1944), p. 55 and *passim;* Fritz Machlup, *The Economics of Sellers' Competition* (1952), p. 202; Milton Friedman, "Lerner on the Economics of Control," *Journal of Political Economy,* LV (1947), 405-16, *passim;* Robertson, *op. cit.,* p. 509; A. Toynbee, *A Study of History,* V (1939), 35 ff.

text of a particular problem occurring in a particular environment."[24]

It should be noted, in passing that because of the multiplicity of combinations hypothetically open to policy makers, and because of their consequent disposition to feel that making anything like an optimal choice is virtually impossible, policy makers may put forth entirely too little effort to select a combination reasonably close to the optimum (if there be such). Under these circumstances, the implied neglect of theory tends to make for the selection of worse policy and policy objectives than need be the case. This failure to explore available combinations sufficiently may be intensified when, as is often the case, the selection of additional policies and policy objectives appears to be much constrained by the selections already made in different but related connections, because at any moment what can be done is subject to restrictions arising out of past actions.[25]

Third, the usefulness of theory may be restricted by nonavailability of requisite data, by accidents of history, by the manner in which policy evolves, and by other circumstances that condition the formation of policy and the definition of policy objectives. When, although a model is formally complete, requisite data are lacking, its usefulness is limited. When a model is incomplete or partial, its use may result in unsatisfactory answers even though data are available for its application. In either instance the model user is in danger of being misled, much as was Carlyle's historian who sought to read "the inscrutable Book of Nature as if it were a [synoptic] Merchant's Ledger."[26] Recall to mind those who, anticipating a postwar depression in the United States, sought

[24] See Meade, *op. cit.*, pp. 108, 117 and Mathematical Supplement (1951), *passim;* also H. G. Johnson, "The Taxonomic Approach to Economic Policy," *Economic Journal*, LXI (1951), 821, 826-30.

[25] See Joseph J. Spengler, "The Role of the State in Shaping Things Economic," *The Tasks of Economic History*, The Journal of Economic History, Supplement VII (1947), 123-43.

[26] Thomas Carlyle, *Miscellaneous Essays*, II (1857), 174.

refuge in trade treaties with the Soviet Union; or those who, believing holders of excessive money stocks to be passive and easily controlled, opposed measures designed to mop up these excess stocks. It sometimes happens, even when theory and information are comparatively adequate, that those in a position to formulate policy understand neither the model nor the role of information, or that, if they understand these matters, they still are deficient in capacity to act, with the result that policy is determined by individuals who know what they want and are persuasive. Witness Bryan's achievement of the Democratic presidential nomination in 1896, or Lenin's rise to power in the fall of 1917. It may also happen that, after a policy objective has been loosely indicated, and an implementing organization has been provided for, the shaping of policy is dominated by the extent to which the several units in such an organization form alliances with complementary elements situated elsewhere in the governmental bureaucracy, and by the degree to which these various units can implement their own conceptions of the over-all program of the organization.[27]

Fourth, because of the extent and the unforeseeableness of prospective change and the consequent likelihood that particular functional relationships and formulations derived with the aid of theory will not continue to hold, it is hazardous to adopt a rigid policy on the basis of empirical findings that may become obsolete. Of the circumstances responsible for this unforeseeableness, the unpredictability of specific technological changes is perhaps the most important.[28] It is quite possible also that particular policies may occasion unantici-

[27] See H. A. Simon, "Birth of an Organization: The Economic Cooperation Administration," *Public Administration Review*, XIII (1953), 227-36. On various factors that affected American foreign policy, see E. F. Penrose, *Economic Planning for the Peace* (1953).

[28] See I. H. Siegel, "Technological Change and Long-Run Forecasting," *Journal of Business*, XXVI (1953), 141-56; A. F. Burns, *The Instability of Consumer Spending*, National Bureau of Economic Research, Inc., (May 1952).

pated and undesirable side-effects and that policy objectives may undergo change as a result of men's experience. Because of these uncertainties, it is frequently desirable, irrespective of what policy is suggested by current theory, that policy be institutionalized in forms that are highly flexible and easy to readjust as significant unanticipatable events take place. Both because of these uncertainties and because of difficulties attendant upon the construction of servo-mechanistic devices and their introduction into policy structures, the usefulness of self-equilibrating arrangements, though initially well-founded in theory, is limited. In general, when a situation or environment is dynamic, it is hazardous to rely too much upon static theory for the derivation of policy indications, particularly if the resulting policy tends to be too static, too restrictive of change, and hence unfavorable to that "propensity to variation" which Bagehot described as "the principle of progress" in the "social as in the animal kingdom."[29] For example, under some circumstances, as Schumpeter suggested, monopoly, though economically indefensible on static theoretical grounds, might be defensible on dynamic grounds, and so on.

Fifth, since policy makers must know what consequences are to be expected from given actions, it is essential for them to distinguish relations that are unidirectionally causal from those that are not so. Yet frequently, theory, when applied to available empirical data, does not disclose whether the relations uncovered are unidirectionally causal or otherwise. Under these circumstances, therefore, policy needs to be formulated and administered pragmatically, so that adjustments can continue to be made in policy as long as its realized outcome differs significantly from its intended objective. This may amount to another argument for flexibility.[30]

[29] *The Works of Walter Bagehot,* V., *Lombard Street,* ed. F. Morgan, (1889), 9.
[30] On some of the issues involved see e.g., Guy H. Orcutt *et al.,* "Toward

VI

I have deferred until last reference to welfare economics, that branch of the science that supposedly is concerned not so much with the construction of instrumental techniques of the sort I have included under policy, as with the supply of standards whereby what I have called policy objectives may be appraised. Throughout most of its history, economics was looked upon as a moral science capable of furnishing certain standards for the comparative evaluation of policy objectives. But with the questioning of the Marshall-Pigou type of assumption that individual satisfaction was measurable and that the satisfactions of randomly selected persons of the same race and country could be compared, the standards of evaluation based on this assumption were rejected. With them went certain arguments theretofore used to defend progressive taxation and related measures, to uphold the alleged superiority of some cultures over others in time and space, and still sometimes used, as Frankel shows,[31] to support programs for the transformation of economically underdeveloped societies. It came to be argued, however, that a policy objective was desirable so long as the gains to be had from it exceeded in aggregate amount what constitute adequate compensation of those injured by the accomplishment of this policy objective; and it was suggested that in some instances (e.g., improvements in technology, or in efficiency of factor-use) a change in policy or policy objective tended to benefit so many and to injure so few that it was almost certain that the affected population would be aggregatively better off. These arguments were questioned of course on empirical, institutional,

Partial Redirection of Econometrics," *Review of Economics and Statistics,* XXXIV (1952), 195-213, and Orcutt, "Actions, Consequences, and Causal Relations," *ibid.,* 305-13; also H. A. Simon, "Logic of Causal Relations," *Journal of Philosophy,* XLIX (1952), 517-28.

[31] See S. H. Frankel, *The Economic Impact on Under-Developed Societies* (1953), Chaps. 3-5, 9.

and other grounds. It was also suggested that policy objectives might be appraised in terms of their effects upon a social welfare function that reflected both an individual's well-being and his appraisal of the manner in which welfare is distributed in a community. But this approach was criticized, in turn, on the ground that the relation of the social welfare function to the welfare of the individual cannot be appropriately specified, and that when more than two alternatives exist, it is unlikely that all the available alternatives will be ordered by the various individuals in such a way as to make a consistent welfare function possible. For, as Arrow has put it, "the possibility of social welfare judgments rests upon a similarity of attitudes toward social alternatives;" and this requisite degree of similarity is unlikely to be encountered in reality.[32]

Let us express our problem in simple but concrete terms. Suppose we have a community of three individuals and that this community is confronted by three quantitatively variable policy objectives, A, B, and C, an increment in the realization of any one of which entails a decrement in the realization of one of the others. Let us assume, therefore, that each individual may combine the variable objectives A, B, and C, in any one of six ways, with any one combination involving less of one objective (say A) and more of another (say

[32] Concerning various of the issues involved see e.g., P. A. Samuelson, *Foundations of Economic Analysis* (1947), Chap. 8; I. D. M. Little, *A Critique of Welfare Economics* (1950); K. J. Arrow, *Social Choice and Individual Values* (1951); Abram Bergson, "Socialist Economics" in *A Survey of Contemporary Economics,* ed. Howard S. Ellis, I (1948), 412 ff. and K. E. Boulding, *ibid.,* II (1952); A. C. Pigou, "Some Aspects of Welfare Economics," *American Economic Review,* XLI (1951), 287-302, and T. Scitovsky, "The State of Welfare Economics," *ibid.,* 303-15; S. Moos, "Laissez-Faire, Planning and Ethics," *Economic Journal,* LV (1945), 17-27; Sir Alexander Gray, "Economics: Yesterday and Tomorrow," *ibid.,* LIX (1949), 510-30; Jerome Rothenberg, "Conditions for a Social Welfare Function," *Journal of Political Economy,* LXI (1953), 389-405, wherein additional recent literature is cited; and Duncan Black and R. A. Newing, *Committee Decisions with Complementary Valuation* (1952).

B or C). On the assumption that each of our three individuals selects at random one of these six combinations, the chances are only 1 in 216 that the same combination will be chosen by all three. Even so, no problem would confront the community if it made no difference to any one individual what combination was chosen by either or both of the others, or if, upon the choices having been discovered to differ, two of the three choosers agreed to accept the combination selected by the third. It is when neither of these solutions is available, and a single solution is not imposed upon all by some individual or some minority or some external agency that the problem of social choice arises and there is needed an arrangement under which individuals are enabled to proceed from a situation in which they disagree respecting the policy objective to be chosen, to a situation in which they agree sufficiently to adopt a common objective, or in which those who do not really prefer the objective most frequently chosen nonetheless acquiesce in this choice.

Despite the difficulties that stand in the way of making social welfare judgments, what purport to be such judgments are continually made in societies, and either are accepted or are acquiesced in. Political theories characteristically and economic theories occasionally are born of man's desire to modify situations he believes to be improvable.[33] Hence, the welfare problem is not likely to be eschewed. Welfare economics, together with related social-science theory, has an important office to perform therefore. It may be expected to throw light upon the establishment of the areas within which decisions are sought. It should be able to provide better answers than we now have to a number of questions concerning the decision-making and related processes by which the choice of policy objectives is dominated at the several levels (ranging from the individual through the various

[33] See Sabine, op. cit., p. 4; A. B. Wolfe, Conservatism, Radicalism, and Scientific Method (1923), passim.

organizations and subcultures with which the individual is identified to the community and its culture) at which selections are made. How numerous and extensive are these processes? How do they operate? To what extent, and under what circumstances, do they favor some unduly at the expense of others and in contradiction with the indications of welfare-economic and related theory. Under what conditions are these indications relatively well complied with? What roles are played by force, other sanctions, ignorance, hypocrisy, tolerance, and so on? To what extent is the selection of divers policy objectives decentralizable to the level of subcultural groups and organizations under circumstances such that what choice is there made produces little effect outside the group or organization in question? Given answers to these questions, policy objectives would come to be selected in greater consonance with the dictates of welfare-economic and related theory than at present. Given more acceptable and presumably more clearly defined policy objectives, theory might be employed with greater skill than it now is in the innovation of suitable policies.[34]

VII

Now, by way of conclusion. After emphasizing the need to define policy operationally and to distinguish it from policy objectives and administrative machinery, I proceeded to show how theory had influenced and might have influenced policy formation in the past. Then I indicated limitations to which the use of theory is subject. Finally, I called attention to past and prospective contributions of welfare-economic and re-

---

[34] Cf. H. A. Simon, "Comments on the Theory of Organizations," *American Political Science Review*, XLVI (1952), 1130-39; Rothenberg, *op. cit.*, pp. 396 ff. and the still-to-be published Shils-Danfield paper cited in *ibid.*, p. 405; also Joseph J. Spengler, "Sociological Value Theory, Economic Analyses and Economic Policy," *American Economic Review*, XLIII (May 1953), 340-49.

lated theory to the selection of policy objectives. In general, I argued that theory should play an important role in the accumulation and analysis of relevant information and in its subsequent application to the definition of policy objectives and the formation of policy. But I noted also the shortcomings of our present theoretical apparatus and the great dearth of concrete and precise information to feed into this apparatus.[35] It follows, in so far as our analysis is valid, that experimentalism, emphasis upon the short-run, and retention of flexibility and freedom to change must continue to characterize policy formation in an important degree. It follows also that, though long-run considerations must not be disregarded, courses of action that greatly emphasize either resort to long-run and rigid approaches, or the centralization of policy prescription and decision-making, are very likely to be beset by hazard.

[35] See F. A. Hayek, *Individualism and Economic Order* (1949), pp. 33-91. But Cf. L. R. Klein, "The Use of Econometric Models as a Guide to Economic Policy," *Econometrica*, XV (1947), 111-51.

3

Economic Objectives in a Changing World

FRANK H. KNIGHT[1]

IT SHOULD HARDLY be necessary to apologize for a superficial and unsatisfactory treatment of this subject, in a public lecture of an academic hour. Another embarrassment I confront is the feeling that so much of what I can say will be things that should hardly need saying; they come close to "triturating the obvious." Like Shakespeare's Mark Antony, I come to tell you that which you yourselves do know, which has a bit the character—to mix scripture—of wasteful and ridiculous excess. What our situation seems to need is not so much science or philosophy that go much beyond common-sense as it is the determined effort at intelligent discussion, avoiding prejudice and easy answers to hard questions. As you will see, I assume that the "objectives" of my title are those of public policy, not of private affairs. And I assume that they relate to a democratic society, where the government that enacts and enforces laws should and must represent public opinion and do the "will of the people." Our own objective on such occasions as this is to contribute a mite to the formation of a more intelligent public opinion. That, however, begins with the *effort* to be intelligent, which suggests exhortation and preaching as much as argument. It is a principle that everyone formally accepts, but that seems to be dishonored in the breach as conspicuously as it is honored in the observance in what passes current as discussion of public economic policy.

[1] Professor of Economics, University of Chicago.

I

The task of defining concrete objectives is at once too easy and impossibly hard. The most general objective of policy in our democratic society is two-fold—freedom with order. Other objectives are rather a matter of detail or clear implication. But the nature of the problem comes out as soon as we ask, how much freedom and in what connections and how much order and how it is to be achieved and maintained "in a changing world." The question could be fully answered only by a code of laws, which must largely be a tissue of compromises; and for these no formula can be given except to use judgment and get the best result possible under the conditions, which must be taken as given until they can be changed. A logical attack on the problem might start from the phrase "a changing world," as a general view of it is the task of intelligently controlling social change. Then, we should have to analyze social change under a cross dichotomy; conceivable changes would be divided into those that are either inevitable or impossible and those that are more or less subject to control, and the latter category divided into those to be considered respectively "good" and "bad."

But there is no clear distinction between ends and means, particularly because the "freedom" objective is obviously both. Intelligent action thus calls for knowing the possibilities of action and their "consequences" and for *comparing* the possibilities, including inaction or letting things take their "natural" course, all in terms of some standards or social ideals, which must also be known. An obvious requirement for social action, implied in knowledge, is general *agreement* on all these matters, and for democratic action this means *free* agreement; and that in turn means intelligent agreement, through open discussion. The "historical" situation in which we find ourselves at the moment is a general movement away from the more extreme individualistic libertarianism of the recent past "backward" towards the statism of an earlier period. It represents a reaction against a reaction; and a major objective now is to keep this under control and prevent it, in turn, going too far.

The only changes that should present issues or are intelligently at issue are such as either reduce freedom or threaten social order. Order is a "categorical imperative," prior even to freedom. Freedom is to be restricted only in the interest of other ideals or objectives, where these actually conflict with freedom, and where or in so far as they become actually more important. Common usage employs the word "justice" to cover the main ideals that are felt to conflict acutely with freedom. But justice may be taken to include freedom, or may even virtually be defined by freedom, as will be shown. In fact one of the main difficulties, and a main point in controversy, is the definition of these concepts and a determination of the range of coincidence or of conflict between them.

Our topic here limits us in a general way to "economic" freedom, and to economic or "distributive" justice. But the term "economic" is another the definition of which is difficult and controversial. It suggests the further objective of *efficiency* and its relation to both freedom and justice. Production is one condition of having something to distribute more or less justly. Increased production is one form or aspect of *progress,* another objective, in which the relation between the economic and other aspects is a very intricate and controversial problem. In fact progress—improvement, desirable change—is an inclusive term for *the* objective. It may cover both ends and means, and its definition calls for some common denominator of its many components. Policy must decide where these are in conflict, and the point at which any one becomes more important than others, wherever more of one is to be had by sacrificing something of others. But this decision, again, is a matter of judgment since none of the components are "measurable" in any strict sense of the word

—not even those we call economic, and the others are even more "imponderable."

Obviously, this is an impossible task. Yet democratic society must solve the problem somehow, and reach a working agreement about it, if it is to carry out any policy or even to continue to exist. If no agreement is reached through free discussion, one must be imposed by force, and then society ceases to be free; and in the absence of agreement either free or forced, society itself ceases to exist, breaking up in chaos. The problems admit of no definite solution, no real "answer," because no one possesses the necessary knowledge in the various fields. Primarily in point are on the one hand the various social "sciences," economics, political science, and history— finally all of them, which must provide information as to the possibilities and consequences of action; and on the other hand, the "normative" disciplines that deal with standards or ideals—chiefly morals or ethics. It is superfluous to remark that in all these fields there is acute disagreement and controversy, among the specialists as well as the general public. More serious than real intellectual disagreement is the fact of controversy—so many think they know and devote their energies to trying to "put over" their view on others, rather than to inquiry aimed at reaching agreement on truth or right. The worst feature of the situation, however, is that so much of what passes for discussion does not reflect the preliminary requirement—a serious effort to be objective and relevant. Undoubtedly the greatest obstacle, the worst enemy, is dogmatism or absolutism. There are no "answers," but some answers are better than others—or at least some are worse. That is the first fact to be recognized. Many hard questions have to be answered, for better or worse, not dismissed as unanswerable.

We cannot expect "perfection" in man or the social order. The concept has no practical meaning, especially for a society committed to freedom and progress. It is an open door inviting to dogmatism, which is the worst enemy of discussion, seeking the best possible compromise, which is the only "formula" offering any hope of agreement. The social ideals that are to direct intelligent action toward desirable change—progress—must undoubtedly be redefined as they are pursued and achieved. For moral progress in that sense—improvement in ideals themselves—is even more important than reaching any ideal that can be set up as a final goal. All pursuit of improvement must constantly have in mind the unalterable conditions of human life on this earth. The ideal must not be allowed to become a barrier to achievement of the best possible, as it constantly tends to do. For it is patently impossible to formulate, to agree upon, any ultimate ideal—perfect men in a perfect society; and we *must* have agreement, and free agreement if we are to have free society. For reasons that I shall try to bring out, people generally have a *prejudice* against compromise, in favor of "sticking to principles," but the heart of the matter is that principles conflict, as well as interests. The favorite principle of moralists "do right though the world perish" is actually a prescription for the "war of all against all"—unless, at least, there is an absolute authority to say what is right, which is the antithesis of free society.

These observations lead to others, chiefly of a negative sort, and therefore disliked as opposed to the craving for definite and positive answers. The channels of discussion "must" be kept open; and above all, *education* must be kept "free." As free as possible, that is. For here extremes meet, the notion of freedom runs, in a way, into its opposite. Education must be undogmatic; no faction or sect must be allowed to get control of it, to use it for indoctrination of any dogma, moral or intellectual. But there is one respect in which the young must be and will be indoctrinated, in one direction or the other, i.e., for or against indoctrination itself. They must be "conditioned," in the formative years, either to regard truth and right as ideals to be pursued, and progressively redefined in open discussion, or else to regard some particular truth and right as established once for all, as given and immutable. But the latter is the worst form of the fallacy of perfectionism. For dogmatism inevitably implies and demands an *authority* to interpret and enforce the particular dogmatic system, and the position of this authority will inevitably be the first and principal cause in the eternal and immutable law itself. I shall say more about this, and illustrate the fact, when I come to consider freedom and democracy in terms of their origin and history.

Prior to that, there is another paradox to be noted, a "quasi-absolute," an exception of the sort that proves the rule and illustrates the general problem. It has to do with the meaning of "society." For the purpose of action, of policy, society means political society. The state is the agency or form through which a society acts and in particular makes and enforces law. In the actual world, the supreme unit is the national "sovereign" state. Again, ideals must bow to realities. Whatever we may say or think about the "brotherhood" of all mankind as an ideal, the nation-states are "there" in the scope and form in which "history" has actually drawn the map of the world and made the constitutions—more through brute force and accident than any rational discussion of ideals. That situation will not be radically changed, for the better, and by tolerable methods, in any foreseeable future. As with other given conditions (given until they can be changed for the better) we have to accept them and work in terms of what exists, while also working for such improvements as seem possible and to be had at tolerable cost. Whatever one may think about the independence of physical reality from perceiving minds, it is pretty clearly absurd to talk about values apart from minds that appreciate them. For us, and as far as we have any way of knowing, the latter occur only in civilized human society, and this in turn only in states. Furthermore, the values we think supremely important depend on the preservation of our own type of state, responsible government through free discussion and representative institutions.

Thus we arrive at the fateful point where an end does justify practically any means really necessary—the practically absolute objective of "defense." I must not digress to consider the difficulties of definition or its baffling relativity, the anomalous fact that nearly all wars are defensive on "our" side, aggressive on the other side, hence logically or illogically both on both sides. Or that loyalty—in our day national patriotism, which was once called the last refuge of a scoundrel—has again become the synonym of virtue, with the power to make virtues of persecution and deception, treachery and murder, otherwise the worst crimes in the calendar. Pacifism is perhaps the outstanding example of the clash between lofty ideals and the necessity that laterally makes virtue of its own requirements, inverting the common meaning of morality. For it is surely self-evident that no state could tolerate a movement or propaganda consistently opposing war, if it were strong enough to be dangerous to the "objective" of national self-preservation. At some point, the principle "my country right or wrong" must be enforced and those who refuse to accept it excluded from influencing the determination of policy. The question is, at what point; and that is the hard question in most issues of conflicting objectives.

In our system of accepted values, this reasoning does not, indeed, justify physical torture of nonconformists, as it was thought to do not far back in our own culture-history—in some relation to the accepted supreme end of the eternal salvation of souls. Perhaps I should say it did not, until recently, with the coming of the iron-curtain situation and cold war. For the headlines of nearly any newspaper furnish disquieting suggestions that man is still a persecuting animal, after the few generations in which we have had a social order based on freedom of discussion, implying the largest measure of toleration of opposed opinions. Incidentally, the "heresy" in question is not legally a crime; established authority is against making it such—because it would make the culprits harder to catch. We have not come to the point of killing them. As has been said, we do not burn them, but merely "fire" them, which may go far toward making it impossible to earn a livelihood for themselves and their dependents. I mention these unpleasant things as a reminder of the terrible difficulty of the problem of policy determination when issues become acute and take the moralistic form. One condition of freedom as a basic objective is toleration of a wide range of disagreement, with preservation of the discussion attitude. The channels of communication must be kept open, as long as "possible;" i.e., until a decision is actually imperative—or the society is fairly agreed in thinking it is. Then the society must act as a unit, if not freely, voluntarily, then under the compulsion of the rest of it by some dominant part, and so ceasing to be free, but with the alternative of ceasing to be a society at all.

Freedom is no absolute—and neither is truth, as I hope later to show more in detail—though truth, defined by freedom of inquiry, is the distinctive and ultimately basic value of free society. To the problem set by the clash between freedom and order—a unitary order in and for the existing social unit that must decide and administer policy—no formula gives any solution. Such a discussion as the present can only point out, quite abstractly, what constitutes intelligent social decision. The "first commandment" is, *compare the alternatives* "objectively," which presupposes that of knowing what they actually are, all that are significant. This procedure "must" lead to a working agreement on the ends of action and the appropriate means, for achieving the "best" compromise among the various conflicting objectives. The "must" is no assurance that it will happen; that is "on the lap of the gods," or of "history."

Here I think a warning or admonition is in place, for us here who, I assume, are members of the "intelligentsia" of our own society. We, at least, must look at problems objectively, impersonally, intelligently, and not in "moralizing" terms. For believers in democracy, it is surely "stupid" to denounce or criticize public officials in power for giving the public what it wants and demands. Or to abuse those who are trying to get positions of power for using the "arguments" that will and do win the votes—as long as it is done in open competition. Similarly, it is stupid to denounce business for producing the goods that are in demand, or selling these by the arguments that will and do have that result. Free society in all departments, politics and business, and propaganda in both fields—finally education too, which lies in both—must be governed by the general principle of demand and supply, both taken in the sense of open competition, with the pro-verbially "sovereign" consumer as the final judge. Freedom to persuade the consumer, in free competition with other persuaders, is of the essence. Moral denunciation may have some effect, but in most cases seems at least to throw the functions in question into the hands of people who are in-different to such treatment. Freedom of expression is the basic freedom, to which the various freedoms of action are rather corollaries. There are limits, of course; there are always limits. Society must have laws defining and punishing fraud and duress, and these must be backed up and supplemented by a moral public opinion. Still further, there must be many other laws and regulations, setting limits to freedom, even freedom of expression, as we all know. The scope of such laws is the general problem of policy, which I shall discuss more con-cretely, as time allows.

At this point, I wish to introduce a "philosophical" obser-vation. In an ultimate analysis a root problem is the relation between error and sin, how to treat these respectively. As a glance at our history will show, this has been a crucial practi-cal issue in western political thinking since its beginning among the Greeks. As you will recall, Plato's Socrates held that virtue is knowledge, while the medieval system made the identification in the opposite direction, treating error as sin—at least as to "heresy," which was the arch-sin and was made to cover sin in general. Modern liberal culture attempts to discriminate the two, and so lands in our worst difficulties, the much-touted crisis in our intellectual and political life. The point here is two-fold: First, only error is discussible; when a question takes the form of which party is wicked and which is righteous, the only recourse is to force. But as always, secondly, there are limits: there comes a point where error *is* sin, or must practically be treated as such. Actually, the current tendency is rather to handle aberrations by diagnosis, as a mental defect or disease. Still, the treatment may not be so very different; and the underlying problem is that of how far the appropriate treatment is open to discussion, with some hope of general agreement. In any case, issues must be kept at the intellectual and discussible level as far as possible. A corollary is that the field in which agreement is considered necessary must be given the narrowest possible boundaries. Social action by democratic process requires agreement, and that is hard to secure.

Man is clearly by nature a disagreeing animal, and conceited, opinionated, and contentious. He is also of course a selfish animal; and the relation between conflicts of interest and differences of opinion is a fundamental aspect of the general problem. But I do not think that wickedness is the main root of social conflicts. Human nature in general does not seem to be basically evil, in a positive or active sense, though the medieval view was to the contrary. People are "honest" enough in thinking that they demand only their "rights." The trouble is rather that their opinions as to what they have a right to are not impartial, relative to conflicting rights and to the possibilities. They are *prejudiced,* and prejudice is hard to classify between error and sin. It is not sin in any conventional meaning—though I for one am far from clear as to what is or was the scriptural meaning of the word.

In any case, when I look concretely at actual disputation over economic policy—our main concern here—the issues often seem to arise neither out of any intellectual disagreement nor out of conflicts of self-interest. I am more puzzled by the frequency with which people vote for policies that are most directly contrary to their economic interests as well as to those of the community: for instance, the traditional "protectionism" of the farmers of the Middle West, where I have lived most of my life. Further illustration may be found in two other perennial bones-of-contention in our economic politics —monetary inflation and arbitrary fixing of prices. Surely one indisputable objective of policy is not to do palpably wasteful and foolish things.

As to protective duties on imports, all that there should ever have been any point in saying has been said long since, over and over, and its validity admitted—and ignored in action. It was well put a century ago in Friedrich Bastiat's famous mock petition of the lampmakers, demanding a law prohibiting windows in houses, to exclude the cheap foreign light from the sun, which was ruining their business. The logic of the case is simple. An American producer does not compete with the foreign producer of the same article, but only with the American producers of whatever goods are exported to pay for the imports. Obviously, the production of one good to exchange for another is simply a choice of a more efficient way of using resources to produce the good received in exchange (or to produce a more valuable good that could not be made directly). The fact that the other party to the exchange is a "foreigner" has no more to do with the case, with any American economic interest, than "the flowers that bloom in the spring, tra-la"—except as it may introduce a prejudice that may be appealed to by those who wish to build fences against the competition of more productive methods.

As to inflation, everyone knows, and most will protest, that it is simply one of the worst possible methods of taxation; and

the alternative—any more defensible method—is too obvious
to need pointing out. Yet governments go on inflating, and
as politicians responsible to the public will, they cannot do
otherwise. Arbitrary price-fixing is in the same class as to its
intelligence. Surely no one needs a course in systematic
economics to teach him that high prices stimulate production
and reduce consumption, and vice versa. The obvious consequence is that any enforced price above the free-market level
will create a "surplus" and one below it a "shortage," en-
tailing waste and generating problems more complex than
any the measure is supposed to solve. Incidentally, any real
problem in the case could be dealt with by unobjectionable
policy. But we have a farm program that at great cost sub-
sidizes waste and helps largely people who have no claim to
public assistance and for the most part at the expense of
people who have a far better claim.

The advocates of such policies however, are honorable
men, wise and honorable, and will no doubt with reasons
answer all I am saying. The explanation of such actions is
neither error nor sin, in any legitimate or accepted meaning.
It lies deeper in human nature, the thing we must understand
if we are to come intelligently to grips with the problem of
social ends and means. I am in the habit of observing that it
is well named, being conspicuously contrary to "nature" and
human only in the denotative sense of what "homo sap"
thinks and does, but without any consistent connotative meaning. Man is a rational animal; yes! he admits it; he says so
himself, thinking it a compliment. And he *is* rational, sometimes, and in varying degree; but he is far more distinctively
irrational, the "romantic fool" of the known world. He also
says he is a social animal, and it is true: he is a natural gang-
ster, partisan, sectarian, and "xenophobe,"—on occasion a
"xenocide," a completely new word to illuminate the idea
of progress. But everybody is social within some circle or
circles and antisocial across the line, with the negligible ex-

ception of a few anchorites, if there are any in the world
today.

Logically, the mystery of the economic policies just mentioned is no more why they are adopted than it is why they
are not carried further, even to completion, if the principles
are sound. Why not prohibit all "foreign" trade, between nations, then between smaller political divisions and communities, and finally stop all division of labor and exchange. In
the currency field, why not print enough money and distribute
it freely to make capital and all wealth a free good and in-
augurate utopia at a stroke—as in fact some of the best minds
have advocated and some would do today, if they believe what
they say. As to prices, why not by law put them all high
enough to satisfy the sellers and at the same time low enough
to suit the buyers, i.e., make them at once infinity and zero?
I could cite public pronouncements, from highly respectable
sources which clearly imply just that. I often ask myself
whether there is any hope of teaching people, if they need to
be taught, that we are all consumers and all producers, and
consequently, there can be no conflict of interest between producers and consumers as classes. I think how fortunate it is
that people commonly act much more sensibly than they talk.
But the fact sets a problem for teaching and for lawmaking,
which have to employ verbal communication.

Mentioning human nature is a reminder that our whole
discussion ought to have a long historical introduction. Everything that is the product of history, and of evolution, and it
is true in a peculiar sense of man, individual and social. Orte-
ga y Gasset merely overstates a profound truth in saying that
"man has no nature: what he has is . . . history." History is
required for understanding the present. But a more important
point here is that in one view the problem of social action is
that of directing the future course of history and specifically
of institutional change, but the men and the society that are
to do so are themselves the product of institutions, of history,

and back of history, of evolution, biological and cosmic. We ought to consider evolution, as a phenomenon of "emergence," in which new levels of reality appear but typically do not replace the old, but rather are superimposed on it. Thus it is necessary to adopt a pluralistic interpretation of man and society as they now are. We should compare and contrast our society with earlier forms out of which it has arisen and on back to "primitive" man, and also with animal societies. The latter exist in two radically different forms, the insect colony and the flocks or herds of the higher animals. The former are interesting in that, like everything else in nature, especially every aggregate, the complex is an expression of law but in a very different meaning from our laws. As far as we can tell, the member units obey the law automatically, mechanically; there seem to be no conflicts of interest between them or between a unit and the society.

Man is not descended from that type of life, and the members of the gregarious animal society are much less strictly or mechanically law-abiding. There clearly are conflicts of interest, often leading to fighting. But still, there is no explicit provision for enforcing the laws that make a society out of the individuals, and still less any such activity as lawmaking. This always means law *changing;* all talk about the origin of law among men, or of the obligation to obey the law is an example of romantic nonsense. There has always been law, and its evolutionary changes are simply one view of the development of things as we see them. A "contract" forming a society out of pre-existing nonsocial individuals is most unaccountably absurd.

We ought particularly to consider the evolution of interests and values, for our problems arise out of conflicts between values, and the social objectives in terms of which conflicts are to be resolved are to be found in values or ideals which must necessarily be the same for all. A primal mystery of man is the fact that as far back as any knowledge can be carried, he lived in a society, a legal order, but disliked obedience to its laws, so that we find institutional machinery for enforcing them. A central feature of this machinery was "myth, ritual and religion," which sanctified and sanctioned by fear of the supernatural whatever was established, supposed to be divinely given, eternal and immutable, and right. It was right by definition, since custom was the only standard of right. Entirely apart from what we may think about "truth" in religion, or other merits it may have, its historical social function of making people obey their laws hardly supports the view of man as a rational animal. For elementary "gumption" should make anyone see that an association of any form or for any purpose must have rules, hence that whatever rules exist (and there always were rules) must be obeyed until they can be changed, and for the better. Karl Marx, as we all know, called religion the "opium of the people," and the jibe fits the sociological facts. Where Marx went wrong was in failing to see that if men will not voluntarily obey the law, something must make them do so, and in so doing put up with much "injustice." The doctrine of the Communist Manifesto, that to achieve an ideal society calls only for a violent revolution destroying all pre-existing social order, is diabolical as well as absurd.

Moreover, an objective view must recognize that only the mysterious workings of history set up the sacred moral principles of Christianity as working rules for a continuing society. Such was not the original intention—most certainly not for a democratic society. Consider the golden rule in relation to slavery. To do as he would be done by, the master should offer to exchange places with the slave; but that would hardly improve the institution! So with the "love of neighbor" principle; it does not tell one how to vote, nor even how to treat people in personal relations in an institutional situation taken as given. It does not instruct a mother, however devoted, what her crying baby needs. It clearly will not do to act towards others in the way that will please them most. We must strive to be just, even when it means being personally "unkind," and must use judgment and courage as to what community life requires. It all comes in the end to our oft-repeated statement, obey the law until it can be improved. Objective examination of our religious-moral precepts or counsels, in their historical context, will show that this conformity (without thought of progress) was in general their intended meaning. In a democracy we must add conscientious participation in enforcing the law and endeavoring to promote progress by improving it.

In our historical background, it was in the Greek city-states, primarily Athens, that men—a very few—first began to be somewhat critical of their established forms and ways of doing, to think of these as not necessarily final but subject to possible improvement. The Greeks did not have the idea of progress in anything like the modern form, but they (a few individuals) did talk, and publish writings, about the good society and the good life, not wholly in defense of things as they were. Though they gave us our word "democracy," their states were not democratic in our sense. Society was based on slavery, the citizens were a hereditary class, and women kept virtually in servitude. The good life, for Plato and Aristotle, was parasitic—contemplation and politics in a state small enough for all citizens to meet in an assembly within the sound of one man's voice. Their freedom was short-lived. They were soon swallowed up in the authoritarian empires of Macedon and then of Rome. Still, what I have pointed out as the basic freedom, that of the mind, prevailed within wide limits, notably a high degree of religious toleration, which continued for some centuries under imperial Rome. Then came the great reaction, Gibbon's "triumph of barbarism and religion," with the conversion to eastern mystery cults and the domination and extermination of these, or the others, by Ecclesiastical Christianity.

The social order of the Middle Ages in western Europe

exemplifies the most extreme authoritarianism, hardly matched in history before or since, under the Church of Rome. It called itself "Christian," though Jesus and the apostles would not have recognized it or accepted any kinship of its position with their teachings. It was notable especially for repression of the "basic freedom" by torture and execution for heresy, defined as questioning its own plenary authority—over "faith and morals," i.e., belief and conduct.[2] The system culminated in the "Holy Inquisition"—logically and inevitably, given its premises and the power it succeeded in acquiring. The "Renaissance and Reformation" replaced ecclesiastical authoritarianism with that of national states under autocracies ruling by divine right, no more "liberal" than the Church had been, in fact less so as to the conditions of the time. Meanwhile came an age of terrible wars of religion, in which none of the protagonists believed in or wanted even religious toleration, not to mention general individual freedom. Circumstances, however, forced these absolutisms into more liberal policies; need for the sinews of war compelled them to accept trade and science, the twin ferments of modern individualism. The next high point was the Enlightenment or Age of Reason —it was in fact as distinctively an age of feeling—marked on the political side by the American and French Revolutions. Its early history is found in seventeenth century England. Then gradually came "toleration," and general liberation of the mind, and with this the liberation of economic life (trade and industry) and political democracy. Thus history, the modern equivalent for God, moves in mysterious ways its wonders to perform, while "men do otherwise than they intend."

The new gospel of "liberty, fraternity and equality" was carried to an impossible extreme in the nineteenth century doctrines of the Classical Economists—following Bentham and Ricardo rather than Adam Smith and culminating in the

[2] Those interested in the history might consult J. B. Bury, *A History of Freedom of Thought* (1952); or read Lord Acton on the same theme.

stark individualistic utilitarianism of J. S. Mill's *On Liberty* and Herbert Spencer's *Social Statics*. Ricardian economics led logically to the social programs of Marx and Henry George; in fact Marxism may be viewed as a "marriage" of the romantic political thought of Rousseau with the confused economic theory of Ricardo. All this led in turn to a new reaction—in the English-speaking world to the socialistic and labor movements, the welfare state, new and newer "freedoms" and "deals." The idealization of human nature was found to have consequences only "less worse" than the doctrine of its hopeless corruption by original sin. Actually, it was the new and "higher" standards that made conditions in the factories and factory towns "intolerable." They were not objectively worse than what had prevailed before but had been explained or taken for granted as "the will of God."

As the basic objective of my discussion is a candid reminder of the facts of history and human nature that finally underlie our problems, what I have said about the irrelevance of our traditional Sunday-school morality to social problems should have as a counterpart some mention of the romanticism and absurdity of many doctrines and pronouncements of Enlightenment liberalism. I, for one, cannot see how anyone of normal adult mentality could ever have believed that all men are born equal, in any meaning relevant for social policy, or that individual liberty is the natural state of mankind. Unless, perhaps, equality means all being equal to zero, and freedom means absolute helplessness and dependence—and for adults rigorous control by institutions and authority backed up by superstitious fear. I recall that the semi-sacred Declaration of Independence was promulgated by and for slave-owners and that slavery was an integral feature of the freedom to which the signers pledged their lives, their fortunes, and their sacred honor. Slavery, incidentally, is a good illustration of the limits of discussion as a political method and the arbitrament of war as the ultimate and sometimes necessary recourse, and an illustration also of the limitations of our religious morality; for when it became an acute issue, in this country, scripture was quoted on both sides—and at least as logically by the proponents as the opponents of the institution. Our then largest churches were "split wide open" and are still struggling to heal the schism. Moreover, we are still haggling over the brutal racial discriminations left in the wake of emancipation.

With respect to literal objectivity, specifically on statements of objectives, historical reminders should not ignore the more realistic document, our federal Constitution. Its preamble, which all patriotic Americans are supposed to know by heart, lists a half a dozen governmental objectives, more or less directly involving economic issues. They are not "absurd" properly interpreted in their context; but none are stated concretely enough to guide action on any issue, or in a way to suggest the obvious conflicts and the problem of compromise. Specific mention of the basic freedom—of thought and expression—came only as an afterthought in amendments, the Bill of Rights. None of the thirteen states had democracy in the sense of universal and equal suffrage; this came gradually and much later, completed by the abolition of the sex qualification only after a world war against despotism. Nothing was said about education—unless some implications are read into the prohibition of religious establishment—and as I have noted, nondogmatic education, available to all and even compulsory within limits, is an "absolute" if somewhat paradoxical requirement. Did the Founding Fathers see the necessity of a genuine separation of church and state? or did it occur to them that sectarianism could be a fine basis for "faction," one of the things they dreaded?

As a matter of fact, Enlightenment liberalism, specifically extreme economic laissez-faire, still evaded the issue of the possibility and necessity of intelligent mass political action in a positive sense and on a serious scale. In principle it works out to much the same thing as a society based on inherited status, a policy of "sitting on the lid," the policing of an ultra-simple pattern. Merely preventing one person from inter-fering with the freedom of others is still preventive action, like that of preventing change of status, the practical social objective of the medieval system, even though the concrete "right" protected by law under liberalism is just what the earlier doctrine denied. The latter establishes freedom but refuses to recognize and face the issues, the conflicts of in-terests, and differences of opinion about values, which inevit-ably arise out of the nature of free society and demand positive social action.

II

At so long last, after skimming over background and ante-cedent conditions, I turn to skim over the crucial issue, the conflict between freedom and justice. The present threat to our society and civilization arises out of a growing bipartisan line-up between interest groups and doctrinaires, one side "howling" for one of these noble principles, the other for the other. Again, my main interest must center in the quality of thinking and discussion, or what passes for such, exem-plified in the controversy on both sides. All I can attempt here is some clarification of the problem, chiefly by pointing out that both parties commit essentially the same error—or "sin"—for as I have said, prejudice and wishful thinking are hard to classify. The advocates on each side define their slogan word in such a way as to swallow up the opposed objective and make their own cover all that is good. Thus each begs his case instead of discussing the composition of the social good as a proportioning of elements partly harmonious and partly conflicting. The hard fact at the bottom is that neither ideal, in any defensible interpretation, can be approximately achieved under the unalterable conditions of human life, even at the sacrifice of the other. Carried to extremes any simple ideal becomes self-defeating and self-contradictory. But the form of the problem of definition is very different for the two concepts at issue here.

Freedom is an element in the social ideal-truistically, for a society committed to it. Whether it is an element in "justice" is a verbal question, but justice should practically need definition only as it conflicts with freedom, itself correctly defined. In a matter of linguistic usage, we clearly need especially to think of history. Originally, as the word shows, justice was defined once for all by the existing positive law. *Jus,* of course, is Latin for law in the general sense, or legal right, a particular being called *lex.* Other modern west-European languages have two words here, but not English. I wish to use "law" in a very broad meaning, to include the whole moral law as well as that part of it which is enacted or enforced by governmental agencies. Not too far back in primitive society, *morals,* custom or the *mores* were the only law and (as I remarked before) the meaning and sole standard of right. For a society such as ours, which has developed (very recently, historically speaking) to a more advanced state, where men question the rightness or justice of existing standards of justice and can speak of unjust laws, we surely ought to use a distinctive word. I would propose to specialize ethics to this notion of an evolving standard by which established law and institutions are to be judged. As improvement or progress is the issue, this would be the name for justice, as the norm for guiding change in legal and moral norms. It properly includes freedom as a component, conflicting more or less with other components. But for the present purpose, it is convenient to stick closer to ordinary usage, and somewhat arbitrarily define justice as the other components of the ideal and be able to speak of the conflict between that and freedom.

The first question for very brief notice will be the definition of freedom. Of course we are not concerned with the metaphysical problem; the freedom in question is the opposite of coercion, not of determinism. In short, as a definition, the correct one is that of Spencer—which goes back to Kant and many legal philosophers, even to Aristotle. Freedom in society means the absence of interference with one's choices by others; it means association by mutual consent, on terms freely agreed upon—with the right not to associate if mutually satisfactory terms cannot be found. Freedom is the right to do what one wishes to do and can do—without coercing others. It presupposes that men have ends and some control over means, and it is relative to the facts, whatever they may be, as to both of these. To the extent that either the wish to act or the ability to act is wanting, freedom is without content —empty, ineffective. For these reasons, freedom is not to be identified with justice, since an individual's ends may be "wrong" or he may lack access to means to which he may have a right—a "just" claim. All that is beside the point in defining freedom, but not in defining justice. Freedom axiomatically implies that the individual acting will take or get the consequences of his own acts. That is essential for a scientific analysis of distribution in economics, but again must not be taken as the meaning of distributive justice. What I am saying may seem to identify freedom with economic freedom and view the whole problem of conduct in economic terms, and I should warn against such an interpretation. The necessity of brevity, and the fact that most choices have an economic aspect, makes it impossible to discuss the subject fully in the present allowable compass; but the tendency to include everything in economics is a major source of fallacy in the discussion of economic policy. As I have noted, there is no clear line between ends and means, and freedom is both; and there are other objective values, along with individual desires, in means as well as ends, in production as well as in consumption.

Economic freedom can only be defined factually as non-interference with the privilege or opportunity of the individual to be the final judge of his own ends or values and of the way of using means to achieve them; or, as a right, freedom is this right. The "economic objective" is merely to use means as effectively or efficiently as possible, for whatever end is chosen. Economic theory considers association only as specialization and exchange for the purpose or objective of increasing efficiency—the product of given means measured by individual ends or preferences expressed in choice in the market. However, efficiency is not all of life. I am reminded of a story or quip about a business efficiency expert who was somehow led to comment on the game of football. His first suggested improvement was to put all the men on the same side instead of having half of them pushing and scheming against the other half. This theme ought to be followed out; for in a realistic view it is apparent that both business, which sets our problems of economic policy, and politics, which must deal with them, are largely competitive sports, perhaps as much as they are instrumentalities for meeting needs or satisfying wants. Consequently, playing the game according to the rules and improving the rules in the interest of a better game are two important aspects of the problem of values for the guidance of policy.

If we believe in economic freedom, the first and indisputable function of government is to protect individuals in their free economic activities, especially their access to the market. For a free market is the only possible form of organization for securing freedom to all in both consumption and production. The main objective of the teaching of economics as a science (in the sense in which it is a science) is to make that proposition generally understood. But a second and no less important objective is to make clear the limitations of the market organization with respect both to its serious mechanical imperfections as it works in reality and its more profound limitations with respect to values other than freedom where these conflict with freedom; and, we should add, where other values conflict with efficiency. For the history of the west in the century or two of liberalism has sufficiently demonstrated that freedom does lead to an astounding increase in production.[3] Freedom of exchange on a large scale inevitably establishes markets, for consumable goods and services and for productive goods and services, and so in general leads to the enterprise organization of economic life. The ideal market of theory embodies the most complete freedom, since any individual confronts equally good opportunities (or infinitely near to equality), so that no one is in a position to dictate terms to anyone else. A market is simply a provision for the public making of offers to exchange on particular terms (prices) giving to each potential buyer and the seller the opportunity to close with the offer that is most advantageous to himself, hence mutually advantageous to both parties. Market relations are not really "competitive" except in the figurative sense that opportunities of choice are competitive. "Rivalry" is extraneous to economic motivation—as, incidentally it is in theory to political activity where in reality it is much more conspicuous. In the theoretically ideal market there is no "bargaining and higgling;" and there is very little in real markets, as anyone must know who cares to look at the facts. Common usage, to the contrary, is another illustration of prejudiced thinking. Calling it theoretically ideal does not imply that it is ideal in a social-ethical sense; that question must be considered on its own merits.[4] The ambiguity of the term is unfortunate, but we must use language as we find it.

The general resultant of the theoretically ideal enterprise of economic organization would be to enable each individual participant to use his given resources—his personal productive capacities and his productive property—in such a way as to

---

[3] The cultural and even moral-humanitarian advance is just as clear, but is not within the province of this paper.

[4] Cf. "ideal conditions" in physical science.

secure the maximum achievement of his given ends that is possible through free co-operation with other individuals. It is a truistic corollary that the share of each in the distribution of the product of the economy would be his specific contribution to the total "social" dividend, the addition made to the total by the employment of the resources individually furnished. All this is mathematically demonstrable, and quite simply; denial reflects confusion of thinking due to prejudice. People who do not like the result of the process as they see it operating repudiate the theory, without asking either how far the reality diverges from the theoretical picture (necessarily much simplified) or why, or how far the conditions that a general theory must take as given are either ethically ideal or unalterable—practically the same thing. A descriptive economic science supplementing the pure theory should answer the first of these questions and provide the foundation for critically answering the second. A supreme merit of the system is that it works without argument, specifically argument about ultimate values or "justice"—where agreement is so difficult and improbable. These questions must be faced, but it is imperative to keep them separate from the theoretical mechanics of economic organization as co-operation for mutual advantage, by given individuals under given conditions.

An especially confusing prejudice appears in the sharp distinction popular in policy discussion between labor and property, or between human rights and property rights. A very little objective inquiry, starting from the truism that property rights *are* human rights, would make it clear that there is no important difference in principle, mechanically or ethically, between the two classes of productive capacity. In any case, both factual differences and their social-ethical implications should be discussed on their merits.

Free enterprise, which is the meaning of free economic organization, leads to distribution on the basis of individual performance—in economic jargon, marginal productivity. The

fallacy on the side of the "howlers for freedom" is identifying this with the social-ethical ideal or justice. The corresponding fallacy on the other side, that of the "howlers for
justice," is that of defining freedom to include all rights,
specifically the right to some access to and control over means.
This may refer to direct means, the consumption goods necessary for some standard of living to which the individual may
be said to have a right, or to the indirect means, the productive capacity necessary to produce such goods. Both
"rights" have validity, up to a point; but it is mere confusion of analysis to define them into freedom. This is done,
consciously or unconsciously, for propaganda purposes, to
capitalize on the prestige value of the notion of freedom in
our common thinking. It has a certain plausibility because, as
I have already stressed, freedom *is* freedom to use means, and
without some control of means, it is empty of content. Nonetheless, freedom and power are different dimensions of voluntary action, the scope of alternatives of choice actually open
to the individual or other unit.

The fallacy is perhaps best brought out by a little consideration of the third of the famous "four freedoms," freedom
from want. I must pass over the fact that none of the four
is self-defining or free from major necessary limitations,
and the list makes no mention of any of the economic
freedoms; and some others that really are freedoms, notably
the vitally important freedom to marry and procreate, producing individuals with rights to be met only at the expense
of other people. The list itself of course was a war manifesto
—like the Declaration of Independence!—rather than political science or philosophy; and criticism might be tempered
accordingly, since in war "all's fair." In any case freedom
from want is no freedom; it means the right to consume without producing, implying coercion of somebody else to do the
opposite thing. That is the antithesis of free association. This,
I repeat, does not deny the right in question, but its nature

and extent ought surely to be discussed on the merits of the policy issues raised, and not begged by an indefensible definition. Up to a point, the right is platitudinous, since the claim of destitution and misery to relief and the obligation of society, ultimately the state, somehow to supply it, have been recognized without question throughout modern history.

But freedom-from-want, stated as a social imperative, without reference to definition or limitation or method of provision, opens the door to assertion of claims and policies that run into the impossible and the fantastic. The consequence, if not the intention, is to make political action a matter of offering the highest bid for the votes of the "disadvantaged," or "forgotten men," identified by themselves or by self-appointed spokesmen. It invites anyone who is dissatisfied with the results of economic competition in production and exchange to resort to political competition and try to get his claims met by voting the right ticket, i.e., to use the power of the government for personal or group or class advantage. I have cited one policy result—our current agricultural program—and need not name others that will occur to anyone disposed to look at facts. These unpleasant things are mentioned because the first requirement of intelligent policy determination is straight-thinking and because of the tremendous obstacle set by the crooked thinking so largely exemplified in public discussion—if the name can be applied to label-pinning, guilt by association, play upon emotion and prejudice, and the like. I am not sure whether these things are morally better or worse when the appeal is to naive idealism, in a way to direct attention away from alternative consequences and from the realistic possibilities.

Here I would turn from negative considerations, from pointing out palpable fallacies and prejudices, to attempt a brief survey of economic policy in somewhat more constructive terms. This might start from our assumed commitment to the ideal of freedom, to be limited or departed from where conflicting values become more important; and specifically as to departure from the free-enterprise organization, which anyhow is with us here and now, as it is, until it is changed, so that the problem is changing it, for the better. A treatment logically falls under two heads: first, the need for social action—politico-legal action—to preserve and increase economic freedom by "making competition more effective," and second, policies required to supplement or replace free-enterprise wherever politico-legal action offers reasonable assurance of improvement—enough better than what is attainable under the first type of policy to justify the costs and risks involved, and to justify the inevitable impairment of freedom, which is not only a means but a value on its own account. We must not forget that even technically "better" government may have to be balanced against and compromised with "free" government. On the other hand, words like "socialism" should be no bugaboo; we actually have "communism" and more so, in education, also in some health measures and others—the commodity is supplied gratis, and the consumer is compelled to take it.

Under the first of our two headings, the mechanical limitations of the market system give rise to policy problems chiefly in connection with the two phenomena, monopoly, and the business cycle. It is impossible here to say much of what needs to be said about either. The monopoly problem is grossly misconceived and exaggerated in the public mind, especially as regards business monopoly, in comparison with others that are even more directly the result of unwise if not positively foolish action by government itself. I refer of course to the restrictionism practiced by or for "labor" and "the farmer," as if either were a homogeneous group, and the two had common interests opposed to any other special interest and justifying public support. Apart from monopoly—and much of that is inevitable and realistically good—the whole idea of a fair price different from the open-market price, is a relic of the medieval status ethics and is an evil in free society. The cycle problem is much harder, and even more patently does not arise out of conflicts of interest, since no important group gains from a depression. The task of its control centers in the field of money (circulating medium) where as in the relief of distress, public action has always been recognized as necessary. But it is hard to act or see how to act very effectively without dangerously restricting basic economic freedoms and freedom in general.

Ultimately far more serious are the policy problems arising out of the limitations of the principle of individual economic freedom. Freedom *means* freedom of individuals, taken as given, particularly—for economic freedom—with respect to their wants or tastes and their possession of means necessary for acting. Controversy centers chiefly on the right to access to means. Too much so; for wants no more than means can be taken as finally given, nor can the right to either be absolute. Both wants and means for satisfying wants are constantly produced in economic life. Obviously, as already sufficiently pointed out, means are necessary to action, and the right to means, direct and indirect, though no part of freedom, must be recognized and made effective up to a point. Without a minimum supply of the means to live—provided by others— an actual majority of the population units would quickly starve. The root of the matter is that society is not made up of individuals, in the meaning of individualistic social theory, economic or political. The majority are dependents, and their interests must be "represented" by someone else. In our society this normally means by the head of a family. The family in some form, and not the literal individual, is the minimum real unit in any society viewed as a continuing entity and obviously the economic unit in consumption and in production. To use words descriptively, what is called "individualism" is really "familism."

Economic analysis must begin by assuming that the unit

has given resources, for this is true at any moment. But it cannot stop with this short-run view. In no very long run most resources, and ultimately all, are produced, have been produced, and have to be reproduced. The stock of all main types must be increased to maintain a given standard of living for an increasing population, and more rapidly if the standard is to be raised. Under familism this providing for the future is left to the free choice of the family, or its individual head who represents it, to save and accumulate in appropriate forms, under the "incentives" that are in fact operative. How far these are "economic" is a question too intricate to go into here. In any case, such decisions are heavily affected by uncertainty, risk, or luck, depending within limits on the knowledge possessed by the decision maker. This luck factor sets one of the hardest problems both for explanatory theory and for the meaning of justice and how to achieve some approximation to it.

Even apart from uncertainty, free or individualistic society presents a strong tendency to increasing inequality, and in ways that run counter to individualistic ideals. Those who at any time possess more reseources are more than proportionately in a position to save and invest and so to accumulate still more. Luck will distort the course of events in both directions, further complicating the problem of justice, or social necessity, and that of social action. As already stressed, society must continue to be a society, and hence must assure some minimum provision for its helpless members—it will not kill them— and must provide for the oncoming generation tolerable conditions in which to grow up into active responsible members. At the other end of the scale, too, "excessive" income or wealth confers dangerous power and leads to many evils. But economic freedom includes freedom both to accumulate and to take chances, while the differential effects, whether due to luck or to differences in capacity or some moral factor, create problems that have to be dealt with through public policy.

One of the most serious limitations of the principle of familistic freedom is that the inequalities arising between parents are passed on to the next generation as an unequal start-in-life, which is a gross injustice by any individualistic definition. The consequence is an acute conflict between the ideal of freedom for one generation and that of justice for the next.

In the interest of justice, and even of social necessity, inequality must be limited; hence the need for qualifying the principle of distribution in accord with contribution, with the rights of accumulation and inheritance or bequest. But this fact in no way establishes equality as a positive definition of social justice. I cannot go into the absurdities of that notion, or the grounds that underlie its sentimental appeal. Sentimentally, I abhor inequality perhaps as much as anyone; but nature has clearly ordained otherwise, and we must "live in the world," within bounds set by our very limited power to change it. Whatever our abstract ideals, moreover, it is self-evident that any group, as a unit, must live on what it produces, and any member unit also, except as some other or others may volunteer, or be forced, to follow the opposite course. Personally, I think that the ideal of justice, as well as necessity, calls for extensive recognition of the performance principle. If "competence" is not a virtue, carrying rights, as well as "good intentions," there would seem to be little point in talking about distributive justice, in a world so radically immoral. And too, our moral sentiments are ambiguous— recall the proverb about the pavement of the road to hell. In any case, productivity must be the basic principle of distribution in a free society, not only as incentive but for guiding the effective use of resources. Finally, other principles must be taken into account—equality, effort or sacrifice, and special needs. But redistribution should be voluntary as far as possible; business *is* business, and charity charity, and the two can be more rationally managed if kept separate—as taxation should be open and aboveboard, not concealed; but, all principles are subject to limitations and exceptions; "circumstances alter cases," and one must "use judgment."

In the determination of social-economic objectives—desirable and possible—in a world that is changing, under possible control to a limited and unknown extent, the wise choice is a matter of compromise and combination among many principles that are valid "up to a point," hence none is "true" in a sense that makes others false. Truth and rationality themselves are subject to limitations and carried to an extreme could make a shambles of society as well as take the joy out of living. More especially, "science"—my time limits have spared you the near-blasphemy of my developing the absurdity of the notion that the problems of morals and politics are to be solved by applying the "scientific method." The socialistic —or is it communistic?—principle attributed to Etienne Cabet: "from each according to his ability, to each according to his need," sounds fine, but under critical examination is romantic and absurd. Yet it has weight, as qualifying other principles. The contrast between sound and sense would be the subject of another lecture. Anyhow, there is a large place in the good life, for the romantic, even the literally nonsensical. In the discussion of social issues the arch sin and the "besetting" one is over-simplification.

4

The Economist and Economic Change

JOHN JEWKES[1]

Anticipation will be assented to much more readily than interpretations, because being deduced from a few instances, and these principally of familiar occurrence, they immediately hit the understanding and satisfy the imagination; whilst on the contrary interpretations, being deduced from various subjects, and these widely dispersed, cannot suddenly strike the understanding, so that in common estimation they must appear difficult and discordant, and almost like the mysteries of faith.

Francis Bacon: *Novum Organum,* Book 1, Aphorism 28

I

SOME TIME AGO I published, in a journal with a specialized and limited circulation, an article in which I pleaded that economists should not claim for their science powers that it did not possess, particularly the power to predict.[2] The economists, to whom it was directly addressed, received it somewhat coldly; which was perhaps not very surprising. Of the few commendations it received, the greater part came from those actively engaged in economic planning, from which I deduced that their experiences in placing whole-hearted confidence in the predictions of economists had not been altogether happy. To me the significant thing was that the article was, in effect, ignored. For whatever may have been in depression in the past few months, there has been a great boom in productive activity. And since I believe that such behaviour is likely to

[1] Professor of Economic Organization, Oxford University.
[2] *Lloyds Bank Review* (April 1953).

undermine the status of economics and the public standing
of economists, which has some importance, and is further
likely to do damage to our economic affairs, which has great
importance, I thought I might take this opportunity of developing further my ideas. My subject can, therefore, be defined as follows: How best can economic science and the
methods of thought that go with it be utilized in further-
ing the aims of the community? In what directions do we find
the best opportunities of applying the accepted principles of
economics and the skills of economists, the formalized understanding and the less spectacular know-how, so that we can
at all times maintain our rights as experts but never permit
ourselves to behave as charlatans? I ought to add, in paren-
thesis, that in my opinion even if economics were completely
useless in the narrow sense there would still be a case to be
made out for its study so long as economists were concerned
with truth and retained their integrity. I see no reason why
they should not, in these matters, be given at least equal treatment with archeologists, astronomers, historians, or philol-
ogists.

II

On the negative side, I submit that economists cannot, without stepping outside their discipline, predict in the sense of
telling us what will happen in the future. It might appear
quite unnecessary to make this point but for the tenacious
hold that contrary ideas now seem to have gained. I listened
the other day to a television programme—it was in this
country but I fear it might have been anywhere else—in
which a group of questioners were taunting a man of public
affairs who also was a distinquished economist: "If you really
are an economist, then predict to us."

The grounds for rejecting prediction as an activity proper
to economic science can be put in general form or displayed as
a series of detailed objections although, in fact, these are

merely different ways of establishing the same conclusion. In the most general sense, there is, indeed, no such thing as the *economic* future. There is only *the* future in which economic factors are bound together, inextricably and quite without hope of separate identification, with the whole universe of forces determining the course of events. This pattern of causes and consequences, even when looked at after the event as history, almost paralyzes the mind with its intricacy. Anyone who proposes to look at it before the event must take as his province the whole of experience and knowledge. He must cease to behave as a specialist, which means that he must cease to behave as an economist.

The economist's claim to predictive authority must be false in that it leads to a palpable absurdity. If the economic future can, indeed, be described, why not also the scientific future, the political future, the social future, the future in each and every sense? Why should we not be able to plumb all the mysteries of future time? Now the economist might argue either that, in his own sphere, he possesses techniques for forecasting superior to those possessed by scientists in other disciplines or that, in the interplay of economic forces, the link between the past and the present and the future, is simpler to understand than in other subjects. But I see no reason for economists to assume that their task is less complex than that of others. Some sociologists, indeed, have claimed that they, too, can usefully predict inventions and technical progress. There are historians prepared to believe that history repeats itself, that by discovering congruent past and present sets of circumstances, the future can be foreseen. I know of no means of disputing such claims by scholars in other fields except by reasoning, which also cuts the ground from under the feet of the economist. It is, incidentally, worth while noting that one group is frequently highly sceptical about the work of other groups of forecasters. In this case a prophet *is* without honour save in his own country.

Even if it be granted that the economist possesses a time telescope, which other students of society have not been able to construct, we are not at the end of the difficulties. The economic future will be determined partly by the predictions themselves. The future then is the compounded result of the economic forces, which would have operated in any case, and the influences exercised by the predictions. The prophets must then be prepared to claim that they comprehend not only the inevitable consequences of current economic forces but also the effect upon the minds of everyone else of what they themselves have to say. There are only two possible lines of escape from this conclusion. It might be said that economists' predictions have *no* influence upon the course of affairs, that nobody listens to them. Scientifically, this might make prediction more respectable but only at the expense of completely destroying its usefulness. The intrinsic interest in making guesses and putting them into sealed envelopes would seem to be small much less, for example, than in picking the winners of horse races without backing horses, and I know of no economist who spends his time in this way. The second escape route, sometimes followed by economists who find their forecasts incorrect, is to claim that the warning inherent in the prediction has been so much taken to heart that people have been led to modify their intended actions and thus have falsified the prediction. Thus it has been said that the scarifying prewar predictions of an imminent, inevitable, and rapid fall in population in most Western countries, predictions generated by or accepted by many economists, have proved woefully wrong simply because people took the appropriate action to avoid the disaster. In my opinion, however, that is not where babies come from. If each time the meteorologist predicted rain this had the effect of increasing or decreasing the rain that would fall, then the virtues of the forecast as a basis for action would be destroyed. That seems to me to be true also in economics.

The weapons that can be employed for economic prediction are two: economic laws, the fundamental logic of the
science, and the facts of the past. Of the first I shall speak in
a moment. As for the second, we can, of course, predict upon
the assumption that past trends continue or have a continuing
momentum of their own, that established regularities will not
change. If such assumptions prove correct, the predictions will
be correct. But if the universe of facts changes, the predictions
will fail. That is to say, the power to predict is most reliable
when it is least necessary, when the conservative rule of
thinking about tomorrow as if it were today is most likely to
be sound. When the circumstances change, on the other hand,
the more strictly the rules for prediction have been adhered to,
the grosser will be the errors.

These general conclusions can, I think, be supported by
glancing at the outcome of recent prediction. First, the forecasts are not always correct. There is no need to enlarge on
this fact. The long list of appalling errors is by now well
known. There are economists in Great Britain and even the
United States who have given the best years of their lives to a
stubborn reiteration of the view that *the* American depression
has at last arrived. Perhaps one of the most extraordinary of
recent predictions was that a shortage of food would be
permanent in the postwar world. If it can be considered a
consolation, the predictions of the sociologists as to invention
and the like have been just as inaccurate as those of the
economists. Of course some predictions do come true. If all
had been wrong, a method of accurate prediction would exist:
to assume that the course of events will be the opposite of the
predictions. On the whole, however, it seems that this per-
verse method would, in the past decade, have yielded many
more successes than have in fact been achieved by economists.

Second, there is evidence to suggest that economists, like
other scientists, are biased—of course unconsciously. I think
it can be established, for example, that economists are on the

whole a pessimistic lot. There are very good reasons why this should be our occupational disease. I consider that it is almost impossible for us, at some point, not to inject into our thoughts about the future, vague impressions that we would not care to defend. Most of us will have gone through that agonising experience of scrutinising a curve of past performance that seems to reveal a trend but that, towards its end, shows some tantalising short period divergencies from the trend; of wondering where the line will go next; of extrapolating on different sets of assumptions; of reaching very different conclusions on the basis of the different assumptions and rejecting the outsize results, without any good reason, just because they are outsize. Perhaps the most famous case is the series of predictions made by the European Commission for Economic Cooperation as to whether there was surplus capacity in the European steel industry. In all such cases, it seems to me impossible that the guesses will not be tipped one way or another by irrelevant factors. On the whole, for example, it is socialists who have predicted most incorrectly about the onset of *the* American depression, and who were most gloomy about the future of Germany, with its new economic policy, until the facts swamped their doubts. On the whole, those who advocate the virtues of free markets have, in their forecasts, been unnecessarily pessimistic about the future of output in Great Britain.

Third, it is clear that different economists looking at the same evidence frequently reach very different conclusions about the future. This is particularly disturbing. It is no answer to say that there are some good economists and some bad ones. It is of the essence of a science that there is a body of universally accepted principles and presuppositions and that, in regard to these at least, all scientists are good scientists.

There are other minor indications of the essentially unscientific nature of these predictions. One is the practice of employing obscure words by which those who use them try to say something significant without being tied down to any statement that can be checked. Hence the evasive distinctions between "depression," "recession," "decline," "re-adjustment," "downturn," and so on. Another is to provide a prediction without a time scale so that the day of reckoning never arises. Another is to claim that whilst predictions about the near future are likely to be incorrect, predictions about the remote future are likely to be right. It is quite extraordinary how many people there are who know that they do not know what will happen next month but appear confident about what will have happened five years hence.

In view of these truisms it may be asked why these predictions continue on such a wide scale. The simple answer is that there is a market, a demand, for them. Nearly everyone of us has to take action that is coloured by our guesses about the future. Certainly every business and every government is in that difficult position, and it is not surprising that they should be prepared to clutch at straws. It is melancholy that men and communities should be exposed to the anxieties and dangers of the unknowable future. But that is one of the facts of life. It is my thesis that, in the last resort, the burdens that fall upon the men of action cannot, in fact, be lifted off their shoulders by economists who hold themselves out as capable of providing a service that they cannot, in fact, perform. On the supply side, economists are perhaps tempted to predict because the risks attendant upon failure are slight, the premiums on success great. A long string of quite incorrect predictions will be completely overlooked if the economist makes one isolated guess correctly. There is a danger, indeed, that a kind of Gresham's Law will operate by which the more spectacular predictions will drive out the less. What is more natural than that an economist who believes that serious economic dangers confront us and who passionately thinks that he knows the way to avoid them, should utter his warnings in an exceptionally strident and alarming form in order to get a hearing at all? There may be a special peril awaiting society just because economists have the interests of mankind so closely at heart.

Although there is little danger of it, in an assembly of this kind, I do not want to be understood to imply that the men who must make the economic decisions cannot derive great and indeed absolutely necessary assistance from those who are trained in ways of economic thought. If I may be allowed to quote from my earlier article:

There is an enormous range of work of immediate practical value to be performed by the economist or the economic statistician, and perhaps only by him, whether he is in a university or is working in close day-to-day contact with men of affairs. Three tasks here stand out above others. The measurement of what has happened in the past and the interpretation of its probable meaning can only be performed properly by those who have developed, by training and experience, wariness and judgment in handling economic statistics, the most slippery of all forms of evidence. Again, there are a number of vital economic mechanisms—banking systems and highly organised markets for money, capital, foreign exchange, basic commodities—about the interconnections of which only the specialist can think and speak with authority. And methods now exist, based upon the concept of the national income, of comprehending the economic system as a whole; these methods, whether they take the form of statistical tables or even of mechanical models, can be deployed to best effect by those who have fully grasped the imperfections and limitations of them. Advice of this kind will fortify the statesman or businessman in judging of the point at which he must depart from certainty and plunge into the relatively unknown.

The golden rule here is that the economic expert should be most scrupulous in setting down all his assumptions and indicating the degree of probability that attaches to each one. The wise man of action, in assessing the importance of the advice tendered to him, will always insist that this is done. For, as a general rule, when economists go wrong, it is not because of any failure of logic but because of some defect in the data or the assumptions from which they start.

My second explanatory word is that I do not deny the value of economic logic. Misunderstanding here is very common because of the different uses to which the word "prediction" can be put. When it is said that *if* the supply of money increases by 100 per cent, everything else remaining equal, prices will rise, no one will demur. If it is declared on such a basis that economists can "predict," there can be no objection, although it would have to be pointed out that this kind of "prediction" is not what I have been talking about. I think it would be better to describe it as economic logic. And there are, of course, a large set of propositions in our logic which enormously increase understanding of the economic world. But we ought to recognise their limitations. When it is said, without any conditions being attached, that if the supply of money increases by 100 per cent next year then prices will rise next year, even then perhaps I would not protest. But with an apology for stating the obvious, I would remind you that we are always uncertain whether the *ifs* will come true; we are always uncertain whether the *other things remaining unchanged* will be true; we are often uncertain whether the *ifs* are really consistent with the *other things remaining unchanged*. We must further recognise that the generalisations of economic logic become progressively less valuable for action the smaller the changes being considered. A statement, for instance, that, if the supply of money increases next year by 5 per cent, prices will rise, is clearly a shot in the dark.

III

I come now to the more positive side of my suggestions. The activities of economists may be misplaced either because they do harm or because they are devoted to less important things before more important things. Both statements may be true, but anyone who makes the second can properly be expected to indicate what tasks, in his opinion, economists are unduly neglecting.

The most important task in economics is that of strengthening and extending the range of economic laws. Difficult as it is even now to define the scope of economics, the subject would become an unsystematic hotchpotch of transient and disconnected interests but for the cohesive power of its fundamental logic. This centralizing body of doctrine accounts for the continuity of modern economic thinking over the past two centuries and explains why so many of the most fertile and subtle thinkers have devoted themselves with such absorption to the subject. Lacking familiarity with this logic, it is almost impossible to escape helpless floundering among the innumerable economic fallacies to which the human mind can be subject.

Despite this there can be no doubt that in recent years the authority of economic theory has declined. The scholars in many important branches of the social sciences related to economics do not even deem it worth while to acquaint themselves with the economist's techniques. Those who make the important economic decisions of the world often brush off the simpler truths of economics as irrelevant or even misleading. The very mention of economic laws arouses generally a restive feeling that some very old, utterly uninteresting, and entirely obsolete incantation is being mumbled. A study of the causes of this loss of prestige would take me too far afield. But there are among them two that are relevant to my thesis.

The first is that the obvious next steps in the development of economic theory present appalling intellectual difficulties. Up to now our economic laws have concerned themselves with static conditions. Although it is true that such laws are in many ways useful and, in any case, are all that we possess in thinking about economic change, it is also true that the speed and ubiquity of technical change, the frequency with which the data alter, make it highly desirable that the element of innovation should be embodied in the system of thought. If, for instance, we concern ourselves with the optimum distribution of economic resources not at a moment of time but over a period, what part of our resources should be devoted to the process of innovation itself? Has economic theory anything at all to tell us about the right rate of investment in industrial or scientific research, or even about the right proportion between the two? Are there rates of economic expansion that, of themselves, provide greater stability in growth than others? These questions have only to be posed to make clear how little we know about them and how difficult it will be ever to theorise about them. Although these are subjects to which some of the best minds in the profession devote themselves, I suspect that the feeling of being up against a blank wall is damping to enthusiasm and confidence.

A second reason why economic theory has lost prestige is, I think, the fault of economists themselves. While they have been searching for a more advanced theory applicable to dynamic conditions and delivering themselves of opinions about the future for which no support can be found in economic theory, many of them have, paradoxically enough, taken the lead in belittling those older and simpler forms of economic logic that, up to now, would seem most reliable and most useful in the framing of policy, It is almost as if a mathematician became so deeply involved in the abstract theory of numbers that he began to doubt that two and two made four and thereby led his poor wife to falsify the domestic accounts. Thus, in recent years, at various times and in various quarters, some economists have argued, or even purported to prove by appeal to facts, that the rate of interest has little or no influence upon business policy; or that the behavior of the business man cannot usefully be studied on the assumption that he is seeking to maximise profits; even that a shortage of the currency of one country suffered by another country cannot be rectified by movements in the rate of exchange. It would not surprise me if, one of these days, some economist comes out with the idea, based on a small public opinion poll, that consumers are not really trying to maximise their satisfaction. These agonising second thoughts about the A.B.C. of their subject doubtless help to explain why economists since the end of the last war have so frequently been reluctant to recommend the processes of the free market, the forces of supply and demand, as the most effective system for correcting economic maladjustments, or restoring economic balance. I very much doubt whether, if action had depended upon a consensus among economists, we would have seen the revival of Germany under their new economic policy, the successful employment of monetary policy as an anti-inflationary measure in Great Britain, or the restoration of much freer economies in other European countries. The attitude taken up at the present time towards the convertibility of currencies seems to me another case in point. There are economists who believe that convertibility will never be possible or desirable, there are others who believe it desirable but who continue to believe that the time is not ripe, there are others who attach almost unsatisfiable conditions to a return to free international markets in currency. There are few who have real confidence in the powers of the market, including the speculative market, to create a balancing system.

The aim of economic science is to reduce the number of uncertainties in a world that, in its totality, will never be knowable. The first function of economists is, therefore, to speak firmly in terms of these certainties they claim to have established. If these claims have, in fact, been dropped, this should be frankly admitted, and we should go into sack cloth and ashes and take up other work. In my opinion, however, the old claims are still good, and economists should constantly be striving to widen the area of certainty in this form, however bleak and difficult that task may seem.

My second suggestion is that economists should become more historically minded both in the sense of devoting more time to studying the work of economic historians (who in my

opinion are far too small a band for the work they have to do)
and in the sense of engaging themselves in historical studies.
No one will doubt, from what I have already said, that I do
not hold history to be a science. But there is a *sense* of history,
a knowledge of the kind of things that *can* happen, a feeling of what fits with what, a comprehension of how a mul-
titude of tiny interlocking events make up the whole, always
possessed by the wise and cultured scholar. I suspect that
what we speak of as economic judgment is a talent of the
same kind, to be cultivated in much the same way. Many years
ago Keynes spoke of this gift when he said "the theory of
economics does not furnish a body of settled conclusions immediately applicable to policy. It is a method rather than a
doctrine, an apparatus of the mind, a technique of thinking
which helps its possessor to draw correct conclusions." Economic judgment is bound up with a sturdy disposition not
to allow current affairs to bulk too large, however insistently
these affairs seem to press upon the mind and the imagination;
with the caution that comes from the knowledge that everything under the sun is both old and new; with the power to
absorb other men's experiences at other times almost as if
they were our personal experiences; with a confidence about
what will probably not happen which remains unshaken
although the future is a dark mystery. You may call this com-
monsense or a sense of the practicable, the feasible, or cool
scepticism, or middle of the road thinking. But it seems to me
most likely to flourish among those who are aware of the
past, and aware of it because they have rubbed up against the
facts of history, sought to place themselves in other men's
minds, watched the frustration of expectations, the occurrence
of the unlikely, the failure of the probable, the collapse of
well-laid plans, and the constant emergence of some new
pattern out of standard and familiar elements.

A closer working contact with history might bring a double
bonus of economic understanding. It would give ballast to

conclusions reached through formal analytical reasoning. Foolish results may, and do, emerge from economic theorising, as a consequence of a slip in one of the steps or neglect of one of the assumptions, unless the theory is steadily confronted with the facts. And it would help to clear up errors about the past. Some notable recent historical and statistical studies have thrown a flood of new light upon the economic events of the past 150 years. Ashton[3] and other writers have shown that the nineteenth century was not the bleak age of falling standards of living, exploitation, and progressive misery that so many had supposed. Stigler[4] and Nutter[5] have thrown serious doubts upon the widely accepted view that industrial monopoly has been steadily increasing since the beginning of this century. Weston[6] has challenged the contention that industrial mergers have, since 1900, contributed greatly to industrial concentration. Adelman[7] has given us grounds for believing that industrial concentration has not been increasing in this century. And the work of Kaplan on the large corporation has provided for us a new conception of the pervasiveness of competition and the precarious hold on the market possessed even by the biggest and apparently most firmly established corporations. It is not too much to say, in view of these results, that a good deal of thinking and writing about the Industrial Age is now obsolete. It is not fanciful to suppose that, if this knowledge had been possessed earlier, Western societies might have been spared much toil and trouble.

There remain many tasks of the same kind. For example, a

[3] T. S. Ashton, *Capitalism and the Historians,* ed. F. A. Hayek, Chaps. 1 and 4.

[4] George J. Stigler, "Competition in the United States," *Five Lectures on Economic Problems* (1950).

[5] G. Warren Nutter, *The Extent of Enterprise Monopoly in the United States, 1899-1939* (1951).

[6] J. Fred Weston, *The Role of Mergers in the Growth of Large Firms* (1953).

[7] M. A. Adelman "The Measurement of Industrial Concentration," *Review of Economics and Statistics,* Vol. XXXIII (November 1951).

study is badly needed of the British economy between the two World Wars. The popular opinion that this was a period of falling standards of living, of decreasing productivity, of backward industries, is palpably incorrect. Again, much more study should be made of the character and the consequences of technical progress, a subject on which opinion swings about in the most puzzling fashion. Up to 1924, it was generally assumed that invention and technical improvement were highly desirable features of any economy, even though doubts were expressed about the distribution of the resultant increase of income or about the more general consequences of a highly mechanised economy. The heavy unemployment in Great Britain after that year and the world crisis after 1930 led to the view that there could be too much technical progress, that it might produce uncontrollable disturbances. The age of "technocracy," however, did not last long. By 1939 the popular theory was that there would probably be too little technical progress. The theory of the mature economy, of secular stagnation, implied that there would not be sufficient inventions to provide profitable outlets for the savings of a community in full employment. Now, in the postwar period, the popular view has once again changed. We are told that technical progress is a guarantee both of improving standards of living and economic stability, that providentially there will never be any shortage of profitable invention, that technical progress has become automatic, that the process of invention has now been invented. These views cannot all be correct. Clearly here is a subject well worth study.

My third and my last suggestion is that there ought to be a rich field for economists, or for some economists since we must have specialisation, in the study, or even the invention if they happened to be gadget minded, of economic institutions, the administrative devices through which economic forces operate and can be harnessed to the best effect. It is arguable that economic progress in the nineteenth century was just as much to be attributed to the discovery and improvement of such institutions—banking systems, the gold standard in various forms, the joint stock company with limited liability, the organised produce markets, the stock exchange, employment exchanges, the patent system—as it was to the brute effect of technical progress. I am not, of course, suggesting that all these ingenious ideas were produced by economists. But economists were closely associated with many of them, and at least they were interested in all of them.

Now I can well imagine some of my listeners hotly denying that economists have lost their ingenuity, asking who invented the budget deficit as a device for maintaining employment, and asserting that ingenuity of that kind is misplaced if not actually wicked. But leaving this awkward exception on one side, I submit that there has been a strange lack of curiosity on the part of economists about some extremely important social experiments of our times. Take, for example, the British National Health Service. The important economic question about that scheme was this: if there is a service the demand for which at zero price is almost infinitely great, if no steps are taken to increase the supply, if the cost curve is rising rapidly, if every citizen is guaranteed by law the best possible medical service, and if there is no obvious method of rationing, what will happen? I do not recall any British economist, before the event, asking these simple questions and, after the event, it is the doctors themselves and not primarily the economists who have raised these questions. Or take the British Nationalization Schemes that, whether they have been good or bad, have been very important institutional experiments. The systematic examination of them, before or after the event, has been surprisingly perfunctory. Or take the very important matter of the relation between the size of, or the degree of monopoly possessed by, industrial organisations and the frequency of invention and industrial development. There are economists (I fear I am one of these) prepared to deliver themselves of generalizations on the subject.

Yet we have practically no systematic knowledge in this field and only a handful of workers interested in it. Or take the patent system: on the one side, it is described as essential for industrial progress, on the other, it is condemned as obsolete. But how much attention have economists devoted to this very important subject in the past quarter of a century?

I find it equally surprising that, although our profession absorbs at least its due proportion of the natural intelligence of each generation, economists have produced in recent years only a thin trickle of ideas for automatically operating schemes and devices as stops and stabilizers in the economy. That point may be illustrated merely by listing some of the main anxieties of our times. It is widely believed that chronic inflation is one of the grave dangers of Western democracies. But where is the flow of bright ideas, from which statesmen could pick and choose, as to how best communities could set a watch on themselves so that they do not thoughtlessly drift into conditions that they will regret? Again if it is true (I am myself doubtful about this but I recognise I am in a minority) that, as between two countries with vastly different levels of efficiency and rates of technical progress, balance of payments difficulties will inevitably arise, have we to assume that there is *no* kind of market for currency that will obviate the need for the State manipulation of trade and currency transactions? If it is recognised, as I think it is now widely recognised, that a Welfare State runs the risk that the more "welfare" provided the more will be demanded and that, ideally, welfare schemes should be automatically self-liquidating, what actual recommendations are before us as to how help can best be provided for the unfortunate in such a way as to destroy the need for such help in the future, as to how "we might emphasise the goal of greater equality in earning capacity rather than greater equality in the distribution of results."[8]

[8] Aaron Director "The Parity of the Economic Market Place," Conference on Freedom and the Law, University of Chicago (May 1953).

If we accept the view that progressive taxation is so seductive a concept that once we start along that course there seems nothing to prevent democracies pursuing it to the point of actual income equality (which few would really like), can economists not tell us where roughly the danger point is to be found and how the brake might be imposed when we approach it? If a budget deficit, properly handled, can assist us in maintaining employment, is it possible to put the use of this weapon into an automatic form that will avoid the confusing political squabbles that will otherwise arise on every occasion that the weapon is employed? Note that the problem in each one of these cases is the same: there are certain changes that are innocuous or even desirable provided they go on at a certain speed and to a limited degree and are not irreversible; but that are disastrous if permitted to exceed that speed or degree and thereby become irreversible. The danger exists so long as the critical points have not been identified.

Now some economists, of course, may not be over worried by the prospect of inflation, of controlled exchanges, or ever-widening welfare schemes, of progressive taxation pushed to its logical conclusion, of increasing national debts through deficit financing. Others who are anxious perhaps comfort themselves with the thought (which I am not prepared to declare foolish) that the worst never happens, that the expected never occurs, that trees do not grow up to the sky. There are others who believe that there is no need for new social and economic gadgets, that the stricter adherence to well-known economic truths and the freer operation of well-tried economic devices should suffice. But I wonder whether there is not something more to be said here. I wonder whether many economists have not in a sense lost heart because they have been driven to the belief that, in Western democratic communities, political forces and the pressure of vested interests are so powerful and can be so blind that the economist, if faithful to the traditions of science, can never do more than whisper in the thunder of an elemental gale. I hope we shall not weary in that way. For in the squalls that drive first one way and then another will always come breaks in the storm when societies must rest to count their self-inflicted wounds and to take stock of those who led them unwisely. In those lulls nations may be inclined to listen to restrained and consistent voices. And therein may be the opportunity of the economists provided, but only provided, that they have not in the meantime allowed their authority completely to lapse by seeking to bluster a way into the ranks of the politicians through making bogus claims for the power of their science.

5

International Trade Theory and Its Present Day Relevance

JACOB VINER[1]

IN AN INTRODUCTION written in 1951 to a collection of some of my articles on international economics, I made this statement about the classical theory of international trade:

> It has in recent years lost its dominance, and its surviving exponents have lost their assurance of its adequacy . . . it needed urgently to have incorporated into it in systematic fashion income propensities and elasticities. But this was well under way prior to the publication of Keynes' *General Theory,* although without use of the terminological labels which it has fastened on economic theory. It seems that the old theory was sufficiently elastic, especially through its monetary phases, to absorb without friction all the Keynesian contributions, and that it is now on the verge of undergoing systematic rehabilitation. Despite my belief in its merits and its relevance during its period of dominance, I am convinced, however, that it would be a mistake to carry its rehabilitation so far as to claim for it, even in its improved and modernized form, adequacy as a theory to guide policy in the present-day world. The world has changed greatly, and is now a world of planned economies, of state trading, of substantially arbitrary and inflexible national price structures, and of managed instability in exchange rates. The classical theory is not directly relevant for such a world, and it may be that for such a world there is and can be no relevant *general* theory.[2]

Dr. Calkins, when he invited me to give this lecture, proposed that I take this passage as my central theme, and that "If you take the position that classical theory is not directly

[1] Professor of Economics, Princeton University.
[2] *International Economics* (1951), p. 16.

relevant, I hope you will suggest what is to be done to analyze problems without it."

In a series of lectures that I gave in 1950 to a Brazilian audience, I tried, in substance, to carry out this assignment, but with specific reference to concrete and current problems of international economic policy.[3] In the present lecture, I shall concentrate on methodological aspects of the problem I have raised. I should point out, however, in abatement of the seemingly negativistic note struck in my 1951 statement, that it was the availability of a relevant *general* theory that it questioned. By "general theory" I meant a comprehensive theory that embraces all the variables recognized as having major significance, which tries to account for all the identified and significant mutual interrelations and dependencies of these variables, which operates with a considerable degree of analytical rigor, and which reaches conclusions that, if true, would be of some consequence. Perhaps if I had made it clearer that my statement referred only to a "general theory" in this technical sense, and not to theorizing, or thinking, in general, it would not have seemed so challenging, and I would not have been invited to give this lecture.

Suppose it be demonstrated, or granted, that there is not available general international trade theory that is relevant either for understanding or for policymaking. What matters it?

I

The great bulk of economic theorizing since it first began to be a professional activity has not been, has not pretended to be, and has not striven to be *general* theorizing. Much of it was so-called partial-equilibrium analysis, where only a very few variables, treated as mutually independent, are specifically taken into account, and all the others, including some identi-

---

[3] *International Trade and Economic Development,* Lectures delivered at the National University of Brazil, 1950 (1952).

fied and conceded to be important, are relegated to the *ceteris paribus* pound, where they are assumed neither to be acted upon by the examined variables nor to act upon them except with over-all constant direction and intensity. Much of it, especially in more recent years, was a search for quantitative correlations between statistical series selected for investigation on the basis of hunches or of partial-equilibrium hypotheses.

Non-"general" theorizing of either of these kinds may be relevant both for understanding and for policy, and much of it, I am sure, has had both kinds of relevance. Its lack of generality was a defect, in that it lessened the reliability of its findings, the degree of confidence that these findings had a right to command, especially when, plausible to the profession in their original time and place, they were applied without adjustment to other times and other places. On the other hand, a theory that is formally indisputably "general" may be without relevance for any time or any place, because the forces, the variables, it recognizes may not be the ones that are in fact important and may even be wholly fictitious and spurious, or alternatively, because such theory may deal with the really significant factors but may attribute to them relative weights or modes of operation that are seriously out of accord with the true state of affairs.

It is an assumption, often left implicit, of the classical theory of international trade that national markets are in their internal operations and, except as interfered with by tariffs, in their international operations as well, basically competitive, that is, free from any important elements of monopoly control. Edgeworth, in 1897, ended a discussion of the consequences for society that would result from a postulated universalization of monopoly with this comment as to its incidental effect on the economics profession:

Among those who would suffer by the new regime there would be one class which particularly interests the readers of this Journal [*Giornale degli Economisti*], namely the abstract economists, who

would be deprived of their occupation, the investigation of the
conditions which determine value. There would survive only the
empirical school, flourishing in a chaos congenial to their
mentality.[4]

Even if I were to accept Edgeworth's assumption, contrary
as it is to all appearances, that the relevance of his theorizing
is a necessary condition of the economic survival of the economic theorist, I would on several counts withhold complete
assent from his position.

First, while I would agree that, in the present state of our
skills, the assumption of competition is necessary for the
prosecution of "general" theorizing, it is not a prerequisite
for partial-equilibrium theorizing.

Second, economic theory does not need to be capable of
producing valid positive findings to have at least a modest
field of practical usefulness, if one grants that the refutation
of pretentious but bad economic theorizing can be a useful
accomplishment. I can here appeal to Edgeworth to rebut
Edgeworth. In an earlier essay, he commented, perceptively,
that "much of our reasoning is directed to the refutation of
fallacies and a great part of our science only raises us to the
zero point of nescience from the negative position of error."[5]
The exposure to the public of ignorant learning is a useful
service, which the economic theorist can perform even when
it is only learned ignorance, awareness of ignorance, which he
can offer in substitution. This is perhaps especially true in the
field of so-called welfare economics, whether in its international trade aspects or otherwise, not because nothing is knowable about welfare, but because the means of acquiring relevant knowledge about it are essentially not the means that
abstract economic theory can provide.

Third, Edgeworth disposes too cavalierly of empirical

[4] F. Y. Edgeworth, *Papers Relating to Political Economy* I (1925),
138-39.
[5] *Journal of the Royal Statistical Society* (December 1889), p. 549.

theory. Empirical theorizing is useful whenever it produces useful results, whether it be with reference to a competitive or to a monopolistic world. Empirical theory, unlike abstract theory, needs to meet only one test, the pragmatic one: Does it work? An empirical theory may seem absurd in the light of an abstract theory, but the embarrassment is for the abstract theorist, not for the empiricist, if the empirical theory works.

Much of the achievement of the natural sciences, I am told, has consisted in the discovery of stable empirical regularities in advance of the discovery of intellectually satisfying theoretical explanations for them, and the empirical regularities have in many cases proved more enduring than the theories that purported to account for them. If we relied on analogy, the same experience could be anticipated for economics, and some of the members of our discipline who must concern themselves about its claims to recognition as a "science" tend to work this analogy hard. Perhaps they are right in doing so. In any case, I hope it was not the systematic searchers for empirical quantitative regularities in economics whom Edgeworth referred to as the "empirical school" to whom intellectual chaos is congenial, but rather the economists of his time who were content to grub around aimlessly in the rubble heaps of unassorted and unrelated facts, neither looking for regularities nor equipped with any tools for discovering them even if they turned up at random. I am sure that if genuine empirical regularities are discovered in the economic world, the theorists will happily embrace them and find a place for them in their theoretical systems.

But how often do economists succeed in discovering genuine empirical regularities even distantly resembling those that natural scientists discover? Findings of empirical economic regularities apparently go stale almost as fast as do eggs, and, even to the empirical economists themselves, nothing seems to be as uninteresting as the discoveries of such regularities by their predecessors. Only one pertinent exception comes to my mind: the regularity in apportionment of expenditures by the consumer formulated as "Engel's Law."

This is skepticism of the fruitfulness of empiricism in economics resting itself on empirical grounds. There are also *a priori* grounds for such skepticism. The success of empirical work in the natural sciences has, as I understand it, consisted largely in the discovery of relatively simple functions that remain stable in form through time and space and have fixed and stable parameters. In some cases the significant variables are very few in number and can be experimented with under strict laboratory controls without loss of relevance for the world outside the laboratory. In other cases the number of operative variables is very great and statistical methods resting on probability theory foundations produce results that have verifiable stability through time and space. In economics, unfortunately, the setting for analysis rarely if ever conforms to either of these patterns. Our significant variables are too many and too interdependent for laboratory isolation and too few, too unequal in importance, too much subject to mutual dependence, to be logically amenable to law of large number techniques of statistical analysis. In consequence we have no logical justification for belief in the existence of important economic functions that are simple, stable through time and space, and characterized by stable and fixed parameters. The social order is in these respects different in kind, or different to so high a degree as for most practical purposes to be equivalent to difference in kind, from the physical or even from the biological order of nature. That in designing our research projects we so often disregard this, is to be explained, I suppose, by the shortage of attractive analytical alternatives, combined with the tendency to justify analysis that proceeds from contrary-to-fact assumptions by claiming for it heuristic value, or the capacity to educe light out of error.

The usefulness and indeed the essentiality of empirical research, including systematic statistical research, when carried on in subordination to abstract theorizing is not in issue. It is only through such research that we can acquire reliable judgments of the dimensions of our problems, of the relative strength of the forces operating to produce them, and of the scale of action needed for their resolution. It is only by means of such research that we determine the external validity, the relevance to reality, of abstract theories of economic mechanism, such as, for instance, theories of mechanism of international transfer of capital, or international transfer of depressions. It is only by such research that we can determine the critical order of dimensions of the various "elasticities" without which knowledge much of abstract theory leads to no concrete results. G. K. Chesterton once said of someone that "he uses statistics as a drunkard uses a lamp-post, for support rather than for illumination." This seems to me to be also the way in which economic theory uses statistics, but it is an important use, for economic theory needs all the empirical support it can possibly get.

My central theme is the question of relevance of economic theorizing. Economic theorists operate, however, in at least five distinguishable "universes of discourse," and for some of these universes relevance to reality has no or little relevance. Economic theory sometimes operates in a universe of intellectual play, without other ulterior motives. Rigor and elegance are here the only relevant tests of workmanship, and internal consistency the only test of validity of the results. Manufactured, predominantly artificial problems will do as well as—usually much better than—real social problems, and any relevance to matters which are of concern to the lay public is likely to be largely fortuitous and exiguous.

Economic theorizing is sometimes carried on largely in a universe of professional tradition, in other words in a historical rut. Here the selection of problems, of assumptions, of techniques of analysis, and perhaps also of pre-established conclusions, is largely determined by inheritance from past teachers or ancient texts. How much relevance such theorizing will have for understanding of current reality or for solving current problems of social policy will of course depend on the nature of the inherited tradition. Even if the past theorizing was fully relevant for the period of its original blossoming, however, and this should not ever be taken for granted, it is in the abstract a reasonable presumption that it will have undergone considerable obsolescence with the passage of time.

Economic theorizing, on the other hand, sometimes operates in a universe of revolt against professional tradition. The revolt may be in the interest of relevance, and may help to achieve it. It may, on the other hand, be merely prejudiced and blindly negative in its motivation and may unwittingly take the paradoxical course of being half-conquered by what it attacks, and of thus preserving vitality for much that otherwise would have been forgotten without loss. Economic theorizing may have as its objective merely or primarily a contribution to understanding of economic process, without assumption of responsibility for evaluating the social impacts of such process, or of proposing either reforms or methods of preserving a desired *status quo*, although the analysis engaged in by one economist in order to yield understanding may help other economists to contribute to policy formulation. Finally, economic theorizing may be intended to be, or to contribute to, problem solving, that is, to provide cause-and-effect analysis and guidance as to appropriate objectives, for use by the economists themselves, by government, or by the public at large, directly or indirectly, in solving social problems, in making things different from what they are, or from what they otherwise would be. This I would label the "action" universe.

It is only for the universe of discourse in which economic theory is primarily an arena of intellectual play that the criteria of "good" theory are primarily "demonstration," "rigor," and "elegance." In the other universes, the criteria are either loyalty to or rejection of traditionalism, or else relevance and probable validity for understanding the real economic world and for improving it.

Since what economists are "kept" to do is to bring understanding of the nature and function of the economic process in the real world both for its own sake and for the contribution that such understanding can make to the fashioning of it into a better world, there is a moral obligation on the part of the profession as a whole, if not on the part of every individual economist, and if not at every moment for any economist, to seek relevance and to assign high value to it. I have no "exclusivist" objectives. Light may come from the strangest sources, and we should not shut our eyes to any of it that comes our way because it has emerged from unexpected sources. The only moral I draw for the individual economic theorist from the argument I have so far presented is that he has two intellectual obligations: first, to seek awareness of which universe he is operating in and to share whatever awareness he attains with his audience, and, second, in his relations with his public, and especially his students and his lay public, to avoid claiming for theorizing, which is governed by sentimental adherence to tradition, by emotional rejection of tradition, or by surrender to play-impulses, anything more than accidental and partial relevance to the understanding of the real world and of the ways in which it can be changed for the better.

Even when relevance is accepted as a major objective of economic theorizing, it should be recognized, moreover, that there are kinds and degrees of relevance, and that it is impracticable and inexpedient for the academic theorist to strain for complete and direct relevance in every detail of his professional activity, and unreasonable to demand it of him. Under different circumstances and for different purposes, different kinds and degrees of relevance are appropriate for the theorist, as, for example, in undergraduate teaching, in training young economists, as oracle to the lay public, or as adviser to or servant of government.

The economist is usually under considerable external pressure to be relevant, or at least to appear to be so, only when he is a civil servant working on specific assignments or participating in the decision-making processes of government. The economist who under these circumstances reveals a lack of concern for relevance is liable to be regarded by his fellow-workers as an unwelcome visitor from one of those ivory towers that universities are supposed to provide on their campuses for their economic theorists as appropriate quarters in which to carry on their geometric or other types of esoteric doodling.

One of the requirements for achievement of relevance is recognition that normally the range of variables significant for the understanding of social problems is a wide one. In governmental policy-making such recognition need not be an individual responsibility, but can emerge as the natural product of a group-process to which all the participants contribute with the aid of their respective skills, stocks of information, and insights. Although there can even then be no assurance that some vital factor is not being overlooked, the activities of interested parties—pressure groups, lobbyists of various species, congressmen, the press, letters from the "public,"—serve to lessen the danger that this may occur.

The academic economist ordinarily works in a drastically different environment, without the sense of personal responsibility, of immediate urgency, and of the importance of detail, which are, ideally at least, operative when statesmen and their auxiliaries are meeting to solve some immediate and specific problem. Nor is the individual campus economist, even on matters in which he has expert competence, ordinarily equipped with the comprehensive and up-to-date information necessary for intelligent solution of immediate and specific problems. All that can be asked of him is that in his teaching, or writing, or research he strive for that degree of practical relevance that is reasonably within his reach and is appropriate to the range of his professional activities.

II

Let me now make some specific applications of these methodological considerations to the classical theory of international trade.

The classical theory of international trade, from Hume and Ricardo to Marshall, Edgeworth, and Taussig, worked as a rule with all of the following assumptions:

(1) the prevalence of full competition both in domestic trade and in international trade except as governments levied import or export duties or granted export bounties;

(2) the existence of sufficient inter-industry and inter-product mobility of the factors of production to result in equal rates of payment and of productivity of specific factors of equal quality in all their employments;

(3) substantial or complete international immobility of the factors of production;

(4) zero transportation costs, internally and internationally;

(5) full employment of all resources;

(6) a universal gold standard, i.e., multilateral "convertibility" in the present-day sense of this term plus approximately stable exchange rates;

(7) monetary and credit systems that worked either automatically or under central management in such a way as to promote smooth and rapid equilibration of international balances of payments;

(8) maximization of aggregate national (or world) real income as the sole pertinent social goal, without reference to the manner of distribution of such income.

It set itself as its chief tasks:

(1) the explanation of the long-run mechanism whereby production was internationally allocated; i.e., the international "division of labor";

(2) the explanation of the short-run process whereby equilibrium in international balances and payments was maintained, or having been disturbed, was restored;

(3) the explanation of the long-run effects on national (or on world) real income of tariffs and bounties and the consequent desirability or otherwise of such measures.

The most striking methodological aspect of the classical theory of international trade, its outstanding claim to originality and genius, was its achievement, practically from its very inception and largely unconsciously and inadvertently, of a degree of "generality" in its analysis that has to this day, I believe, not been exceeded in any other branch of economic theory and has not been reached in any other branch that has made any real effort to maintain important links with reality. The classical theory of international trade was both macroeconomic and microeconomic theory simultaneously, and although it by no means succeeded in identifying and explicitly analyzing all the types of interdependence between variables that could conceivably be of great economic significance, it managed to leave at least substantial room and perhaps complete room in its analysis for these interdependencies to exercise their effect on the final results.

When dealing with exposition of the international mechanism of adjustment, or of international "equilibration," the classical theory subsumed under an elastic formula of interaction between the quantity of money and other mutually dependent variables a wide variety of possible paths of adjustment to a variety of types of exogenous disturbance. It is the practice today to distinguish these different paths to adjustment and to analyze them in isolation from each other.

If the classical approach is open to the criticism of a vagueness that is perhaps not curable within the limits set by its own technique, the modern approach is open to what seems to me to be the more serious criticism of abstracting from both highly significant variables and highly significant interdependencies between variables, both of which abstractions are—or so it seems to me—incurable within the limits of its method of analysis and either of which suffices to convict the analysis of irrelevance to most objectives except the "play" one.

To deal with value and real-income aspects, the classical theory of international trade invented an ingenious concept, "reciprocal demand," or to use a label less likely to mislead, "reciprocal demand-and-supply." It thereby abstracted from the "monetary veil." It thus confined its analysis to "real" quantities, on the assumption that the operations of monetary institutions did not in the long run seriously affect the dimensions of the "real quantities" or the forms of the "real-quantity" functions. It thereby also, by an extraordinary tour-de-force, succeeded in moving beyond the partial equilibrium analysis of orthodox (domestic) price theory, where demand and supply relating to a common market or economy are treated, logically absurdly, as being completely independent of each other, to a level of analysis where the mutual dependence of demand and supply is provided for by fusing the two concepts into one.

No one, not even the originators of these innovations in analysis, has ever given them the emphasis or the methodological scrutiny they very much deserve. They have for the most part been rejected without full understanding or adopted casually, uncritically, and intermittently. The most pregnant comment that I know of on the "reciprocal demand" concept was made by Edgeworth in a single-sentence reference to its geometrical expression:

. . . A movement along a supply-and-demand curve of international trade should be considered as attended with rearrangements of internal trade; as the movement of the hand of a clock corresponds to considerable unseen movements of the machinery.[6]

Whatever the merits or the defects of these methodological innovations embodied in the classical theory of international trade, they are crucial for it, and any departure from either of them, even when made by economists who have elsewhere worked in its framework, takes the analysis embodying such departure outside the realm of what, in the remainder of this lecture, I shall refer to as the classical theory of international trade.

It is my opinion, which has strengthened over the years, that within the limits of the range of problems to which the exponents of the classical theory of international trade chose intensively to apply it, it was in the light of all the contemporary circumstances an eminently successful theory. It dealt with problems that the public and the governments of the time regarded as important. It dealt with these problems with a high degree of relevance and realism in its selection of premises and of modes of analysis. Its analysis had a high degree of explanatory value for current economic process. Its findings provided valuable elements of guidance for social policy. There was not available an alternative body of theory or alternative set of analytical procedures that could have been substituted bodily for it without a great net loss of relevance, of elegance and rigor, and of social utility.

The classical theory has been criticized for not dealing with the theoretical and practical problems arising out of dynamic or growth factors or "economic development"; out of international movement of labor and capital; out of the differences in relative provision of different regions with the different factors of production; out of the existence of transportation costs; out of the existence of fluctuating exchanges; and so forth. It is true, I think, that the theory was never syste-

---

[6] Edgeworth, *Papers Relating to Political Economy,* II (1925), 32.

matically applied to any of these problems, although what the exponents of the theory did say about them has never been carefully surveyed and if so surveyed might surprize by its extent and pertinence. Heckscher and Ohlin have made a notable contribution in extending or revising the classical theory to deal enlighteningly with the significance for international specialization of differences in the relative endowment with the various factors of production of different regions. With this important exception, there has been very little exploration of consequence either of the possibilities of applying the classical theory to the analysis of those long-run problems that it neglected but that now command our interest, or of inventing new methods of analysis capable of handling them with some measure of generality and rigor.

Aside from its inquiries into certain phases of the mechanism of international transfer of capital, the classical theory of international trade, like classical theory in general, did not deal systematically with short-run problems. We have recently had a period in economic thought—I hope, a short-run period—during which there was little interest in any problems other than short-run ones. In any case, the classical theory of international trade was not designed to deal with short-run problems and as a rule has not been applied to them.

Every one is now agreed that the classical theory of the international mechanism either ignored or gave too little attention to income elasticities. It has been an important contribution of post-classical school economists to incorporate income elasticities systematically into their accounts of the international mechanism. As has so often happened, however, in the history of economic thought, recognition of a hitherto neglected factor has been associated with rejection of a hitherto overemphasized factor. In the classical theory, substantially all of the equilibrating work was attributed to price elasticities. In a good deal of modern theorizing either price changes are rejected as a part of the equilibrating process, or price elasticities are declared to be so low as to make the contribution of relative price changes to the maintenance of equilibrium a negligible one. With equilibrating significance denied also to changes in monetary stock, no equilibrating factor is left except income elasticities.

Theorists have always had a predilection for explaining observed phenomena in terms of as few causes as possible. The predilection is often supported on grounds of formal logic by question-begging appeal to Occam's Razor. In the distant past it was often defended by appeal to that dogma of cosmic philosophy known as the "Law of the Parsimony of Causes." Adam Smith explained it as that "propensity" which "is natural to all men, but which philosophers in particular are apt to cultivate with a peculiar fondness, as the great means of displaying their ingenuity—the propensity to account for all appearances from as few principles as possible."[7]

Taussig, struck by the way in which before World War I international balances had remained in equilibrium without friction and without interruption, found it difficult to believe that all this could be accomplished by the operation of price elasticities alone. It was only belatedly that I saw reason for Taussig's puzzlement and that I realized that both the classical theory and the new theory being proposed as a substitute for it had the common defect of probable inadequacy of the assigned cause to produce the observed effect. A story told about the Duke of Wellington when he had become old and rather inflexible has perhaps enough relevance to justify my repeating it. The Duke was telling a junior officer of an experience he had had at an officers' mess during the Peninsular War. A bottle of port had been opened for him, and inside it he found a rat. "It must have been a very large bottle," remarked the amazed junior officer. The Duke fixed him with his eye. "It was a damned small bottle." "Oh,"

[7] Adam Smith, *Theory of Moral Sentiments*, Pt. vii, Sec. ii, Chap. ii.

said the junior officer, abashed: "then no doubt it was a very small rat." "On the contrary," said the Duke, "it was a damned large rat!"

If both income and price elasticities are recognized to be operative in the equilibrating mechanism, there would cease to be occasion, one would think, for skepticism as to its adequacy, at least under nineteenth century conditions. There would then be no obvious disproportionality between the size of the rat and the size of the bottle which contained it. This has not been universally admitted, however, and there have been instances of economists insisting, apparently not only with respect to present conditions but also with respect to the pre-1914 world, that there was not sufficient adjusting mechanism to prevent chronic disequilibrium in the absence of resort to direct quantitative controls by government. Whether or not this makes sense for present-day circumstances does not concern me for the moment. If it is applied, however, to the pre-1914 century, it raises the question of why chronic international disequilibrium did not more clearly manifest itself in that free-market noninterventionist century.

Cannot it be argued, however, that under nineteenth-century conditions there was operating as an equilibrating force, in addition to price elasticities and income elasticities, a third factor, the supply-of-money factor? Let us suppose that in the nineteenth century an autonomous continuing transfer of income had associated with it, whether automatically or by virtue of standard patterns of central bank operation, a relative change in the national stocks of money as between recipient and paying countries, and let us assume further that this change was in the equilibrating direction and exceeded in proportion the initial relative change in regional incomes with which it was associated. In the classical theory all of this was assumed, but the only implication drawn from it was that it would produce a change in relative price levels in an equilibrating direction. In some of the "modern" theorizing, relative changes in stocks of money are either left unmentioned, or asserted not to be part of the mechanism, or claimed to have no or negligible consequences.

The supply-of-money factor could conceivably have been of substantial importance for the equilibrating mechanism under nineteenth century conditions. It would have operated through a number of more-or-less familiar "effects," with respect to willingness to spend or to invest on the part of holders of cash balances and willingness and ability to borrow for spending or investment on the part of others.

There is, first, the effect on interest rates of more abundant or less abundant supplies of cash balances. This has been plausibly held to be of little consequence directly for short-term credit. There are no valid grounds, empirical or *a priori,* however, for denying its importance directly for long-term credit and investment. If important for long-term credit, however, it must indirectly be important also for short-term credit, to the extent that the demand for short-term credit is complementary to, instead of rival to or independent of, the demand for long-term credit.

There are, second, the liquidity effect, including under this the effect of changes in liquidity on willingness to spend, to engage in direct investment, and to make loans available to others; third, the capitalization effect, or the effect of changes in values of capital assets resulting from changes in interest rates on willingness to spend and invest and on willingness and ability to borrow for spending or investment; and finally, the speculative effect, or the effect of the changes in expectations as to future price and profit trends that result from knowledge as to changes in stocks of money that have occurred.

I conclude from all of this that with or without the improvements that new theorizing has brought, there is available an adequate body of theory with respect to the international mechanism that would be relevant for understanding of the real world and for guidance in policy-making if conditions today were still substantially as they were before 1914.

It is much more difficult to meet the modern criticisms of the classical theory of international values, especially in its normative or "welfare" phases, which were its major *raison d'être*. These criticisms constitute a direct challenge to the possibility of attaining any degree of rigor and generality of analysis without totally surrendering relevance. The problems are too many and too complex for adequate treatment here, but I do not pretend that I would have satisfying answers to them even if I were allowed unlimited time, since I know from experience that some partial answers that I have offered leave the critics of the classical theory unconvinced and unimpressed. Some of these problems, moreover, are no more crucial for international trade theory than for economic theory in general, so that it is not a special responsibility of the international trade theorist to find solutions for them. I omit, on this ground, anything beyond mere mention of, among other things, such thorny issues as the need for and the possibility of meaningful "real cost" and "utility" analysis, or of the possibility of the existence of static long-run decreasing costs and their consequences, if they do exist, for equilibrium analysis. I select for more detailed treatment the question of the meaning and the usefulness of geometrical representations of "reciprocal demand" in both descriptive and normative analysis.

It has been objected against the standard reciprocal-demand diagrams that they are limited to two-country, two-commodity models, and therefore cannot have relevance—or cannot confidently be attributed relevance—for a multi-country, multi-commodity world. The objection against the Marshall-Edgeworth type of reciprocal-demand diagram that it is appropriate only, if at all, for a two-country world is, for most purposes, without validity. This type of diagram is never to be interpreted as a two-country diagram supposed to be applicable to a world of *many* countries. It should be interpreted instead as an *n*-country diagram, with the country of special interest, "your" country, set off against all the other countries gathered together into a rest-of-the-world compound. If desired, each country in turn can be chosen for separate examination in a separate diagram in relation to its corresponding "rest-of-the-world." By any one of several available geometrical procedures that involve no change whatsoever in the basic assumptions, all the countries, no matter how numerous they may be, can in principle be separately and simultaneously accounted for in a single diagram. Difficulties arise only when tariffs are introduced, and either more than one country is assumed to have a tariff, or any country has a tariff that discriminates as between two or more other countries.

The objection against the reciprocal-demand diagrams that they can deal *rigorously* only with a world-model in which only two kinds of commodities are internationally traded is valid. The only alternative procedure that has been extensively explored is the arithmetical model. In principle, this is subject to no limits as to number of countries or of commodities, but in practice it not only seems inevitably to be unwieldly and inflexible, but to carry with it implicit question-begging or extraneous assumptions that deprive its results of any serious claim to relevance, except as its use is confined to demonstrating the possibility that a particular proposition *may* have practical validity.

I concede that reciprocal-demand geometry, at least of the types now available, cannot deal with problems arising out of the existence of discriminating tariffs. But as far as I know, this has never been made the basis of criticism. Leaving this aside, I concede also that, without simplifying assumptions of a kind that are liable to be destructive of relevance, we do not know how to demonstrate geometrically the derivation of a reciprocal demand curve from its underlying determinants and therefore are condemned to some measure of vagueness as to the changes in its locus and shape, which would result from changes in the basic assumptions as to cost and consumer-choice functions. Subject to these qualifications, I venture to suggest that the number of countries, the number of commodities, or even the ratio of number of commodities to number of countries, are *per se* of no crucial significance for any theory of international trade problem. Where the contrary has been made so far to appear to be true, it has been the consequence in every case, not of dividing given aggregates of demand into a larger number of sub-aggregates, with respect to areas, or to commodities, or to both, but by changing the economic size of the "rest-of-the-world" relative to a given country and of incidentally and arbitrarily changing the underlying functions.

When it comes to the welfare, or "gains-from-trade," conclusions that the old school drew from their reciprocal-demand analysis, there is ample ground, I concede, for caution in following them without major reservations. The idea, for instance, of being able to determine the optimum level of a tariff by relatively simple geometry on its face invites the type of incredulity that in another connection led Coleridge to ask: "What should we think of one who said that his love of his wife was north-west-by-west of his passion for roast beef?"

The intellectual difficulties that the theory of international trade faces in its normative aspects are common to all attempts at welfare analysis in economics, and recent developments in welfare theory have served much more to bring the difficulties into fuller light than to discover ways of surmounting them by rigorous and abstract methods of analysis. Against complete rejection of the usefulness of such analysis, I can at this time make only a few specific points. First, the analysis can serve to expose the error of or the lack of foundation for some types of welfare propositions. Second, the analysis can serve as a guide to the nature of the information that needs to be gathered, and the type of value-choices that need to be made, before normative conclusions can rationally be reached. Third, the quantitative interpersonal comparisons of "utility" or "benefit" or "gain," which all welfare analysis implies, are not shown to be impossible merely by showing that "measurement" in some strict sense of the term is impossible as far as "utilities" are concerned. Interpersonal comparisons of utility are meaningful as long as a reasonable person would accept them, as a guide to decision-making, in preference to acknowledgment of nescience.

Even in his most confident moments, however, the economist should never think of claiming that as economist and with the use only of economic information and economic tools of analysis he can reach final welfare verdicts. Economic theory tends, probably out of methodological if not psychological compulsions, to conduct welfare analysis in terms of single objectives, assumed to represent simple and homogeneous quantities of welfare—stuff, such as "gain," "benefit," "development," "income," and so forth. Economic theory tends to accept the limitations imposed by a law of parsimony of social goals as well as by a law of parsimony of causes.

In the actual course of policy-making in the real world, however, the monistic concepts that economic theory uses in its welfare analysis seem always to be catch-all labels for complex package of objectives that the policy-maker in practice is forced to separate out and to weigh against each other when they conflict with each other. The concept, for example, of long-run economic "gain" or "loss" with respect to a specific tariff measure has to cover the impacts of the measure on consumer interests, on user-industry interests, on producer-interests, on regional interests, on the national budget. In terms of abstract analysis the reciprocal-demand curves reflect these factors fully. But in order to derive from the reciprocal-demand diagrams specific answers to welfare questions, it is necessary to know not only what the shape and location of the reciprocal-demand curves are with respect to measured ordinates, but also for at least one of the reciprocal-demand curves its relation to the indifference-curve maps for the country to which it refers. I would insist that it is not in principle impossible for the policy-maker, or better, for a policy-making group, to acquire a sufficient quantity of the needed information to make possible a better answer, that is, an answer more likely to be correct, than would be attainable without such abstract analysis plus such factual research. But the geometry provides only a procedure for giving shape and logic to the empirical investigation and not categorical answers to specific welfare questions. It is one of the virtues of the reciprocal-demand technique that since in principle it takes everything that is relevant for economic gain or loss implicitly into account, the task of finding an empirical counterpart for it involves that in principle every relevant kind of fact shall be searched for and given appropriate weight.

It of course goes without saying that man does not live by real income alone, and that noneconomic considerations must and will play a part in the policy-making process. But the responsibility of the economist, *qua* economist, ends when he has brought into the decision-making process the economic facts and the economic objectives relevant to the problem under consideration.

III

The statement with which I began this lecture may well have given you the impression that I had come here to bury the classical theory of international trade, not to praise it. It may therefore have puzzled you that I have instead spent so much time in singing its praises. I have been intermittently warning you, however, that as far as my central issue of relevance was concerned, I have so far been examining the relevance of the classical theory only for a world conforming substantially to its nineteenth-century types of assumptions. My claims for it so far have been limited to the proposition that if the conditions of the nineteenth century were still with us, the classical theory of international trade would still on the whole serve us very well for the problems it was designed to deal with. But our economic world has changed in many respects since the nineteenth century. It is on the basis that these may have been crucial changes for the relevance to the real world of the classical theory, and only on this basis, that I feel myself warranted in raising the question whether the classical theory has sufficient present-day relevance to justify trying to keep it alive otherwise than as marking a distinguished episode in the history of economic thought.

The international gold standard has disappeared and with it have disappeared either exchange-rate stability or free exchange markets or both. Much of foreign trade is now conducted directly by governments, and much of what is still in private hands is subject to a close degree of government regulation through import controls, exchange controls, allocations of raw materials, export subsidies, and so forth. National economies are now over the greater part of the world subject to central planning, where they are not directly operated by government. Price-structures in most countries are no longer overwhelmingly the product of competitive free-market forces, and in all countries contain elements of arbitrariness and managed rigidity. There are no longer any free international markets for either short-term or long-term capital, and access to foreign credit is now to a large extent a matter of *ad hoc* negotiation between governments. The elements of governmental operation, of governmental control, and of private monopoly in market operations are now so important that it has become otiose to assume that in most or even many of the national economies the effective prices reflect closely the relative "real worth" or "real costs" of the staple goods and services. Given the extent and the character of official control of foreign trade, it has become equally otiose to assume that the course of international trade is dominated by the relations among market-determined prices.

Earlier in my lecture I gave a summary account of the fundamental assumptions on which the classical theory of international trade rested. Superficially at least, they seem radically different from the actual conditions under which international trade is carried on today. Is the classical theory sufficiently elastic to be able to withstand, perhaps with some minor amendment, this apparent change in the nature of the world it purports to describe?

In a paper read at the meeting last December of the American Economic Association, Professor Haberler, from whom I have learned much and still have much to learn about the theory of international trade, stands up in defense of the continued relevance of the classical theory under modern conditions.[8] He opens his talk with a quotation of the same passage from my 1951 book with which I opened this lecture, and characterizes the tone of the passage as "unusually mournful and apologetic, and quite atypical."

Professor Haberler claims that I have exaggerated the degree of change since the nineteenth century in the basic circumstances under which international trade is carried on and that there survive much more flexibility and competition in modern markets than my passage would indicate. I have made no careful survey of the facts, and perhaps Professor Haberler is right. I note, however, that in presenting his case for the prevalence of competition, he makes no mention of the Communist part of the world, does not refer to the proportion of the foreign trade of noncommunist countries that is con-

[8] Gottfried Haberler, "The Relevance of the Classical Theory under Modern Conditions," *American Economic Review*, XLIV (May 1954) 543-51.

ducted directly by governments, and in claiming that "imperfect competition" is amenable to international trade theorizing of the classical type, or to a good available substitute for it, overlooks the fact—if it is a fact—that in much of the world cartellization rather than imperfect competition is the dominant form of deviation from the competitive market. Eminent economists, moreover, have seriously questioned the resemblance of the assumptions of the classical theory even to the conditions that prevailed in the nineteenth century.

I believe, however, that what difference there is here between Haberler and myself turns much less on questions of fact than on how much deviation between its assumptions and the facts the classical theory can stand without losing most or all of its relevance. Economic theories, I would concede, are not ultimately problems in pure mathematics even when they are presented in that form, and we should expect them to have some give in their assumptions. But there must be a limit somewhere. A theory elastic enough to withstand almost any degree of subversion of its premises must be a theory so good in general that it is not much good for anything specific.

It seems to be true, moreover, that the "classical theory" whose continued relevance Haberler defends is to a large extent a different body of theory, reaching generally perhaps the same conclusions but by radically different methods of analysis, from that "classical theory" whose past achievements I celebrate and whose present obsolescence I mourn.

The theory of international mechanism whose relevance Haberler defends is the classical mechanism *plus* flexibility of the exchanges, *plus* built-in inflation instead of stable equilibrium as its end-result, plus governments assumed not to use their greatly extended range of activities either extensively or in a manner out of harmony with the requirements of the theory. If governments instead push policies of direct control far enough, Haberler concedes, "the market theory of the mechanism becomes irrelevant and inapplicable." I am willing to leave it at this. In so far as we are here talking about the same theoretical issues, Haberler and I appear to be in substantial agreement.

Another branch of international trade theory that Haberler examines for relevance is the theory of the determination of exchange rates under conditions of flexibility. As he says:

> . . . The theory operates with shapes and shifts of demand and supply curves of one currency in terms of another . . . the curves are derived from demand and supply curves of exports and imports; the latter are ·deduced from demand and supply curves of consumers and producers . . .

This is predominantly a post-classical type of theorizing, and when I use the term "classical theory of international trade" I always intend to exclude theorizing of this kind from its coverage. Such theorizing, by its reliance on national demand curves for imports independent of what happens to exports, of national supply curves for exports independent of what happens to imports, and of supplies of and demands for foreign currencies similarly independent of each other, abandons the search for mutual dependencies that was an essential characteristic of the classical theory of international trade. The "modern" theory of the exchange rates is not for me a meaningful theory, and I see in it no relevance either for the nineteenth century or for present-day conditions. It belongs, I think, exclusively to the "play" universe of discourse. But that is an issue which cannot be settled here.

Finally, as to the present-day relevance of the welfare aspects of the classical theory of international trade, Haberler and I are in agreement that the theory depends for its validity and relevance upon actual prices reflecting "real costs" in some appropriate sense of that term. I also agree with him, if I understand this aright to be his position, that whatever degree of absence of relationship there may be today between relative actual prices and "real costs," the classical theory still has relevance as providing an argument in support of the wish for a world in which the relationship was a closer one. I am also in agreement with him in believing that the classical welfare theory can still be of service in performing the negative function of demonstrating the inconclusiveness of the welfare arguments presented in support of specific programs of trade restriction and of governmental intervention. My Brazil Lectures were in large part an effort in this direction.

There are, I am sure, other aspects of international trade theory on which we are closer together than appears on the surface, but it would probably take joint debate on our part with those who dislike both the methods and the aspirations of the classical theory to draw them fully into the light.

Suppose it to be true that the classical theory has lost relevance for the problems of the present-day world. What then is the proper procedure for the economic theorist? Obviously, he should seek for a new theory, one if possible with at least equal degrees with the old of generality and rigor and elegance, but, above all, one with relevance. This is a familiar plight in other disciplines. What seems to me a striking parallel from the field of hydraulics has been brought to my attention. The classical hydrodynamics, without sacrificing relevance for the practical problems to which it was applied in the nineteenth century, attained mathematical rigor and elegance by postulating an "ideal fluid," which was frictionless and incompressible in its flow, a concept which I take to have some resemblance to our concept of "perfect competition." Unfortunately, however, for the relevance of the theory for modern aerodynamics, it is friction and compressibility of air that account for the ability of airplanes to fly. A new theory, consequently, was urgently required. This has been in process of development under the label of "Hydromechanics" but has required the invention of some new mathematics and the surrender, temporarily at least, in the interest of relevance, of much of the rigor and elegance of the classical theory.[9]

It seems to me that economics must seek the solution of its methodological problems along a substantially similar route. We should first clarify as much as possible the requirements that an adequately relevant theory would have to meet, especially with reference to the assumptions it would have to rest on. We should then appeal to the mathematicians for the sort of help they have been giving to hydromechanics. Meanwhile, we should be endeavoring to make some progress on our own by piecemeal revision of old theory and piecemeal introduction of serviceable innovations as they become available. Until either as the result of a protracted period of piecemeal evolution or by benefit of aid from the mathematicians or from the contributions of some economic genius, a theory at once relevant, rigorous, and elegant comes into our possession, we should reconcile ourselves to even wholesale surrender of rigor and elegance to the demands of relevance, and should be appropriately modest about the claims to reliability of the conclusions we reach.

If there is agreement that relevance is of supreme importance for economic theory, it leads to certain rules of guidance as to the procedure we should follow in constructing our theoretical models. It is common practice to start with the simplest and the most rigorous model, and to leave it to a later stage, or to others, to introduce into the model additional variables or other complicating elements. I venture to suggest that the most useful type of "first approximation" would

---

[9] See L. Prandtl, "Historical Remarks," *Fundamentals of Hydro- and Aeromechanics* (1934), pp. 2-4. I am indebted to Arnold Goldburg, Princeton University, for drawing my attention to the existence of similarities between the methodological problems of economics and hydraulics.

often be of a radically different character. It would consist of a listing of all the variables known or believed to be or suspected of being of substantial significance, and corresponding listing of types and directions of interrelationship between these variables. A second stage of ahalysis would consist of a combing out on the basis of such empirical evidence as can be accumulated of the probably least significant variables and interrelationships between variables. Instead of beginning with rigor and elegance, only from this second stage on would these become legitimate goals, and even then for a time they should be distant goals, to be given high value only after it is clear that they can be reached without substantial loss of relevance.

Such procedure, it would seem to me, would have some distinct advantages as compared to the more usual procedure on the part of theorists of starting—and often ending—with models that gain their rigor at the cost of unrealistic simplification. In the first case, important variables would be less likely to be omitted from consideration because of oversight, traditional practice, difficulty of manipulation, or unsuitability for specific types of analytical manipulation to which the researcher has an irrational attachment. Secondly, there would be at least partial awareness of what variables had been omitted from the final analysis, and therefore greater likelihood than at present that the conclusions will be offered with the qualifications and the caution that such omission makes appropriate. Third, if the presentation of the final results includes a statement with respect to the omitted variables and the reasons for their omission, the reader of such presentation is in better position to appraise the significance of the findings and is afforded some measure of guidance as to the further information and the new or improved techniques of analysis that would be most helpful.

The final outcome of such a change in analytical procedure

might well be a definitive loss in rigor and elegance at least for a long time, on the one hand, but a definite gain in scope for the useful exploitation of new information and of wisdom and insight on the other hand. Such a result, I hope and believe, would in most cases constitute a new gain in relevance for understanding of reality and for the promotion of economic welfare by means of economic theorizing.

6

Freedom and Order

LIONEL ROBBINS[1]

I SHOULD LIKE TO PREFACE this lecture by confessing to you
that I have found it very hard to prepare. As I usually find
choosing a subject a matter of great difficulty and anxiety, it
was with great pleasure that I accepted your invitation to lecture on a topic already predetermined, which seemed to me
both interesting and important. What could be more relevant
to our current problems and perplexities than the relations between freedom and order! But as I came to reflect further,
as I came to read round my subject and to collect on little
slips of paper the stray thoughts that passed through my head,
I began to feel that I had agreed to do something almost beyond my powers; and further attempts to organize my material have only deepened this fear. I am afraid that what I
have to offer this evening must appear extraordinarily sketchy
—a series of notes rather than a systematic treatment, a record
of the responses of an economist to certain general problems
rather than a logical build-up of social theory.

I

Let me begin with ethical ultimates. The words "freedom"
and "order" each appeal to our emotions. When we hear them
said or when we read them, we respond favourably: we feel
that they stand for something desirable. We want freedom
and we want order—at least I do. Arguments on either theme
can command a considerable degree of assent.

[1] Professor of Economics, London School of Economics.

131

At first sight, therefore, it might appear that our central problem, the problem of the relation between freedom and order, was a problem of determining the proportions, so to speak, in which these two goods should be combined. Doubtless on one level that is how it looks. Much of what I shall have to say this evening will be concerned with the limitation of freedom to secure order and of order to secure freedom. There are a great many special problems that can suitably be posed in this manner.

But if instead of describing particular tasks, we are trying to weigh final objectives, then, I think, this way of putting the problem may be very seriously misleading. For, at least as I conceive things, in the last analysis, freedom and order are not on all fours at all. They are not each ultimately desirable states to be combined in a suitable ratio in order to achieve some sort of maximum. Rather they are related to each other as end and means. I desire freedom as an end in itself. I desire order as a means to freedom.

This view is not one that is universally adopted: some of the greatest minds that have worked in this field have adopted positions that are radically opposed to it. It has been denied that freedom is good in itself. It has been claimed that certain kinds of order are intrinsically valuable. It will make my own position clearer if I set out a little the pros and cons of these opposing positions.

Take first the doctrine of freedom as an end. The stock objection to this way of looking at things is the question: *freedom for what?* Freedom, it is urged, is not something that is intrinsically good. It is a condition of action rather than a criterion thereof. A free action is good if it leads to a good end; it is bad if it leads to a bad one.

Now it may be admitted at once that there is a point here that is well made. If describing freedom as an end in itself implied that all free acts were good regardless of their content, the position would be untenable. Clearly some free acts are good and some are bad. It is the main function of moral judgment to make just such distinctions.

But while it would be wrong and, indeed, absurd to claim that all free acts are good, I venture to suggest that it is neither wrong nor absurd to claim that, before any action can be judged to be either good or bad, it must have the quality of being free. An unfree act may lead to good results, as may a shower of rain, or it may lead to bad results, as may an earthquake. But like the rain and the earthquake, in itself it is not a suitable subject for moral judgment.

In saying this, I say nothing one way or the other on the grand question of free will or determinism. It may be that there is a sense in which ultimately nothing is free, although personally I should be a little surprised if this were so. But in the context of social ethics this is irrelevant. We may find it hard to give a definition of social freedom that is totally immune from objection. But we know in practice what it means: or at least we know the meaning of freedom. We know what it means always to look over one's shoulder when one talks. We know the difference between choosing one's own way of life and living the way someone else thinks is good for us. For my purposes that is all we need to know. All that I am asserting at this stage is that only acts that are not unfree in this sense are eligible for moral classification. So that although it would be wrong to regard freedom as being in itself an ultimate good, it is an essential condition of anything that is. The creation of conditions that are free may be the creation of conditions in which good and bad are possible. But unless there is freedom, there is no possibility of good at all. It is in this sense that I speak of freedom as an end. It is in this sense that the prevalence of freedom is a precondition of the good society.

II

Let me now turn to the claims of order. It is not at all impossible to understand the frame of mind in which certain patterns of social relationships seem in themselves to be good. We are moved by the spectacle of order in the universe around us. The mysterious world of aesthetic values, so elusive yet so intensely real, seems to depend ultimately upon the proper ordering of its various ingredients. It is easy to transfer such habits of evaluation to social relationships and to argue that what is good and desirable is conformity to a certain order. Plato's Republic, where the relations between the citizens are supposed to realize in themselves the idea of justice, is an example of this kind of conception. It is the recurrent ideal through history of spirits who are perplexed and shocked by the apparent disorderliness of change.[2]

We must not dismiss such views as ridiculous. It may well be that some sorts of order in adult social relationships are indeed aesthetically pleasing. But as I see things, before they can be the subject of moral approbation—as distinct from the approbation that we give to pleasing natural objects—they must be the result of free choice on the part of those participating. On this view there is all the difference in the world between an order that is *imposed* and an order that is *achieved;* and it is only in respect of the latter that a mature human society can be judged in terms different from the terms in which we judge the state of a herd of domestic cattle. This is not in the least to decry aesthetic values and aesthetic experiences. In the life of the individual they may well be preeminent—revelations of modes of being far transcending in importance the life of the common day. It is only to say that, by themselves, they are not appropriate to the evaluation of

[2] See Karl Raimund Popper, *The Open Society and Its Enemies* (1950), for a masterly analysis of Plato in these terms. My discussion at this point is heavily indebted to this truly great book.

social arrangements. To value social patterns as such, whether or not they are imposed from above or freely achieved, is to commit the ethical sin against the Holy Spirit—to regard human beings as instruments and not as ends in themselves.

It is by arguments of this sort that I would seek to dispose of the purely aesthetic case for order as opposed to freedom. But, of course, even if these arguments be accepted, they do not dispose of the case that can be built up on other grounds. They do not at all dispose of what may be called the utilitarian arguments for paternalism. These seem to me to be much more formidable and to deserve somewhat fuller attention.

The case for liberty as I have presented it involves an assumption that so far I have not made very explicit—the assumption, namely, that the citizens are sufficiently mature to know their own interest or to be guided towards it by reason and persuasion. Even in the most advanced society, the argument for freedom cannot sensibly be applied to the case of children or imbeciles. It would be fairly generally conceded that it does not apply in full rigour to backward adult societies. This point was well put by John Stuart Mill in his classical statement of the case for liberty, who said:

It is, perhaps, hardly necessary to say, that this doctrine is meant to apply to human beings in the maturity of their faculties. We are not speaking of children, or of young persons below the age which the law may fix as that of manhood or of womanhood. Those who are still in a state to require being taken care of by others, must be protected against their own actions as well as against external injury. For the same reason we may leave out of consideration those backward states of society in which the race itself may be considered in its nonage. . . . Liberty, as a principle, has no application to any state of things anterior to the time when mankind have become capable of being improved by free and equal discussion. Until then, there is nothing for them but implicit obedience to an Akbar or a Charlemagne, if they are so fortunate as to find one.[3]

[3] *On Liberty*, Blackwell reprint (1946), p. 9.

The argument is cogent. But it must be recognized, that once it is admitted, there arise very serious problems concerning where to draw the line. Who is to say at what time a child becomes capable of being guided by reason and persuasion? When does a backward race cease to be backward? How certain is it that all adult members of advanced communities are fully capable of reasonable action? This last point, in particular, was seized upon by that very acute lawyer, Fitzjames Stephen and made the basis for by far the most searching attack that has ever been made on Mill's libertarian theory. He said:

> You admit that children and human beings in "backward states of society" may be coerced for their own good. You would let Charlemagne coerce the Saxons, and Akbar the Hindoos. Why then may not educated men coerce the ignorant? What is there in the character of a very commonplace ignorant peasant or petty shopkeeper in these days which makes him a less fit subject for coercion on Mr. Mill's principle than the Hindoo nobles and princes who were coerced by Akbar?[4]

I can think of various answers to this position. It could be argued, perhaps, that the degree of maturity postulated by Mill's contention is not very great; and that although beyond that point paternal control may produce immediate good, yet in the long run it inhibits further development and so prevents an even greater good. I think Mill would have argued this way, and I am sure that in many cases such a reply would be valid.

Nevertheless, if we are honest with ourselves, I do not believe that all of those who take the libertarian view would at all times wish to confine the argument for paternalism to these very narrow limits. Modern governments do many things, which, while not strictly necessary to preserve liberty, yet involve some interference with liberty, at least in the

----

[4] Fitzjames Stephen, *Liberty, Equality and Fraternity,* Second Ed. (1874), p. 28n.

shape of additional taxation; and while we should probably condemn some, perhaps many, of these activities, it is improbable that we should condemn all of them. Think, for instance, of the use of taxpayers' money to finance some form of learning which does not pay for itself or to preserve some historical monument which, if not provided for in this way, would crumble or be disposed of for other purposes. Many of the educational and cultural functions of government often involve a considerable degree of implicit paternalism; and I think we rightly regard as doctrinaire those who are quick to call them in question.

That is all very well. But if we acknowledge such exceptions, the problem presents itself with even greater insistence, where then are we to draw the line? For although we ought not to worry too much about small infringements—*de minimis non curat lex*—yet if we have no line at all in mind, we may easily find that in admitting these small exceptions we have, so to speak, let in the whole theory of paternalism by a back door. I do not think that it is altogether an answer to say that these are problems each of which must be dealt with on its merits by good sense and long-run considerations of utility. That, in effect, was Fitzjames Stephen's answer. But without some additional safeguard, it is very easy to imagine his main argument being made the pretext for extensions of paternalism, which probably he would have been among the very first to condemn.

The right qualification, I think, is one that in fact has been provided elsewhere by Mill himself. In his *Principles of Political Economy* when discussing paternalistic intervention he lays it down that:

. . . In these cases, the mode in which the government can most surely demonstrate the sincerity by which it intends the greatest good of its subjects is by doing the things which are made incumbent upon it by the helplessness of the public, in such a manner as shall tend not to increase and perpetuate but to correct that helplessness . . . government aid when given merely in default of private enterprise, should be so given as to be as far as possible a course of education for the people in the art of accomplishing great objects by individual energy and voluntary co-operation.[5]

That surely is the ultimate test. We can justify paternalism if it can genuinely be said to be a preparation for freedom. We can justify some limitation of present freedom if it can genuinely be shown to be in the interests of greater freedom in the future. There are obvious dangers even here: it is not difficult to think of the most disgraceful acts that it might be attempted to justify in this way. But, in principle, I think the rule is sound. At least it has the merit of involving no derogation from the ultimate case for freedom.

III

Up to this point my remarks have been directed to establishing the precedence of freedom over order in the realm of ends. I have tried to exhibit freedom, if not as something necessarily always good, at least as something that is a condition of good; while I have exhibited order as instrumental. I now reach a stage where the emphasis needs to be changed, where, without regarding order as good in itself, I have to discuss it as an indispensable condition of freedom.

I take it that I do not need to spend much time in establishing the general principle that freedom in society does not mean freedom to do just anything regardless of the effect on others, but rather freedom within a code of rules designed to eliminate disharmonies. It is clear that freedom is reduced if we all consider ourselves free to behave as gangsters. Moreover, there are many forms of activity not gangster-like which if unco-ordinated or unrestrained may lead to loss of freedom. The business of living together involves an apparatus of law

[5] John Stuart Mill, *Principles of Political Economy.* (Ashley Ed.) (1909) Book V, Chap. XI, p. 978.

and order. And the provision of this apparatus and of certain other goods enjoyed in common involves contributions in cash or services in kind that are also a matter of obligation. The framing of such rules and the imposition of such levies in such a way as to create freedom rather than to destroy it, is doubtless a matter of intense difficulty; it is the grand problem of the art of liberal politics. But of their necessity in principle there is no very serious question.

There is, however, an aspect of all this, an aspect that is peculiarly germane to my general subject—which is not always sufficiently emphasized—namely, the essential core of coercion that underlies this apparatus. However much we may insist that the purpose of the state is to safeguard freedom and the good life that freedom makes possible, we deceive ourselves and run the risk of serious practical error if we do not recognize that it is not a purely voluntary association— that in the last analysis it involves an irreducible element of force.

It is worth while dwelling a little on this point, for it is a matter on which some economists at any rate have entertained delusions and fostered constructions that definitely conceal this somewhat unpalatable fact. There are so many social relationships that one can conceive in terms of spontaneous agreement and contract, so many complicated liens that rest entirely upon mutual benefit, that it is tempting to conceive of the state in the same way. It is admitted that we cannot think of the state as a market, giving due proportionate representation to the bids of minorities, however small and however associated. But can we not at least base our conception on the idea of a club all of whose actions are the result of mutual agreement?

Unfortunately this is not so. It is quite true, of course, that there is a sense, immortalized by Hume, in which all government can be said to rest upon consent—somebody's consent, the consent of the persons or groups of persons who have it in their power to make trouble. But it is not true, it never has been true, and it is never likely to be true that all the citizens will obey the law willingly all the time and pay their taxes as voluntary contributions. The idea of a club leaves out the essential distinction between the state and other forms of association. In the old days when migration was freer and when national exclusiveness was weaker, there was rather more plausibility for those contractual theories of government, according to which if you rejected the arrangements of one state, you transferred your allegiance to another. But they were never true for the great majority of the people; and they failed to touch the inner necessities of the situation. It is silly to say that if you hang a man or put him in prison you do it with his consent. Doubtless it should be the aim of all to see the coercive element in government reduced to a minimum, to bring it about that what is voluntarily accepted grows more and more and what is accepted only as a result of *force majeure* grows less and less. Doubtless it is supremely important to bring it about that the exercise of force is not arbitrary, that there exists a machinery for peaceful change of the government and a law (or binding conventions) limiting its scope. But we oversimplify the world and leave out an essential part of the picture if we fail to recognize the irreducible surd of coercion in any conceivable stable society. What is worse, we may compromise the possibilities of freedom.

We can see this very clearly if we consider the present state of international society where there is no one supreme coercive power to enforce the law among states and where in consequence there prevails not order but anarchy. It is difficult to think of anything more vividly resembling Hobbes' description of the state of nature, before law backed by force came into being. Certainly in our modern age we pass our days in "fear and danger of violent death," and the life of man runs the gravest risk of being for this reason "poor, nasty, brutish and short." Yet such is the blindness of a certain form of libertarian outlook that in just such circumstances as these, security is expected to arise from a universal perception of harmony of interests; and restrictions on sovereignty are denounced as restrictions upon liberty. Please do not misunderstand me in this connection. I have no immediate cure-all for the international chaos. I would certainly not support the creation at this stage of a world federation in which the likeminded peoples of the West were hopelessly outvoted by hundreds of millions of people who are not like-minded in this way. I do not even believe in the immediate practicability of complete federation of the Western Powers, although I myself would regard it as the most hopeful thing that could possibly happen in our time. All that I wish to do here is to illustrate the chaos of social life without a framework of law and order and the futility of arrangements that neglect the need for the essential minimum of force. We may not know how to solve our present problems. But it is at least something to recognize clearly wherein these problems consist.

IV

I now approach the heart of the problem—at least as it presents itself to the economist. I have tried to demonstrate the claims of freedom and the general necessity for law backed by force. I have now to ask what kind of order in the economic sphere best satisfies the criteria I have formulated.

After what I have said on the general issue, I do not think that it is necessary to spend much time on the case for freedom in individual spending. To be free within the limits of one's resources to choose between the alternatives both of present consumption and of provision for the future; I will not say that this is the whole essence of freedom, but at least it is an essential constituent. There are of course difficulties in any simple formulas in this field. There is a margin for reasonable dispute in regard to saving and accumulation. There are kinds of desirable services that for technical reasons cannot be restricted to particular consumers—the whole field of indiscriminate benefit—where we have either to go without or be content with some governmental decision involving overriding of minority preference. There are forms of private consumption that have effects on other consumers—the field of the so-called external diseconomies—where unlimited freedom may not be in the general interest. But in the main the principle is clear: the choice between existing goods and the choice what goods should be produced should be as free as possible.

Up to this point the position I have adopted might be shared by many socialists. Socialism in practice tends to the standardization of consumption and the adaptation of people to plans rather than plans to people. But there is nothing in the initial conception that implies these developments; and many convinced socialists would indignantly repudiate any such intention. The idea of freedom in the sphere of consumption is one which may be regarded as common both to liberal individualists and to liberal collectivists. It is when we come to the sphere of production that ideas are radically different.

There are two main arguments against over-all collectivism in the sphere of production—note, please, that I say *over-all* collectivism; I have no desire to argue against all collectivist enterprise or against any conceivable collectivist experiment.

The first is an argument on grounds of efficiency. If the purpose of production is to serve the free choices of the citizens, then it is argued, over-all collectivism must fail in that by its very nature it is unable to decentralize enough adequately to fulfill this purpose. Without the degree of decentralization implied by dispersed ownership and initiative untrammeled by orders from the centre, the system must always tend either to inefficiency in meeting a free demand or to regimentation of demand in order to avoid inefficiency.

This objection can be developed in different ways. It can be based, as it was based by von Mises, upon the difficulty of creating a full market system where the bids of the managers of production are limited to the requirements of a plan that is not of their making. It can be based upon the tendencies to congestion in a system that is necessarily bureaucratic. Each, I think, has a solid foundation of good sense and experience. Properly interpreted, the occasional success of collectivism in particular lines of production or in the organization of a war economy is no refutation but rather a confirmation of this view.[6]

The second argument against over-all collectivism is even more directly related to the central preoccupation of this lecture. It is the argument that collective ownership and control of the means of production is a danger to freedom.

It is important to realize the main burden of this argument. It is not restricted to the fact that the control by the state of the processes of production is itself a limitation of the freedom of those members of society who would wish to undertake productive enterprise on their own. This is a grave limitation, and one which is probably cumulative in its evil effects; in a society in which no one can be free in this respect, it is likely that eventually no one will want to be free—which is still worse. Much graver, however, is the general limitation of freedom for all citizens except the rulers, that must necessarily arise in a society in which there is only one property owner and one employer—the state.

This was well put by John Stuart Mill, who cannot conceivably be represented as being hostile to the beneficent intentions of collectivism.

If the roads, the railways, the banks, the insurance offices, the great joint stock companies, the universities, and the public charities were all of them branches of the government, if, in

[6] See my *Economic Problem in Peace and War* (1947) Lecture II, *passim*.

addition, the municipal corporations and the local boards, with all that now devolves on them became departments of the central administration; if the employees of all these different enterprises were appointed and paid by the government and look to the government for every rise in life; not all the freedom of the press and popular constitution of the legislature would make this or any other country free otherwise than in name.[7]

This point of view can be put too crudely. It is not true that every experiment in collectivism is a grave menace to liberty; it is not true that every country that has nationalized its railways lives under the shadow of totalitarian tyranny—I speak as one who is opposed to the public ownership of railways. But broadly and cumulatively Mill was surely right. The concentration of property under over-all collectivism must eventually be inimical to freedom. Perhaps from time to time the totalitarian night may appear to be lightened by attempts to create freedom by official order. Authors may be told not to be sycophantic, thinkers may be told to think for themselves. But you do not gather grapes of thistles; and where there is no dispersion of power, there freedom must either wither and die—or else itself change the system.

For both these reasons I hold that if freedom is to be preserved and progress assured, we must look outside collectivism for the answer. We must look to a system in which there is truly independent initiative and truly dispersed power. And let there be no doubt as to the reason. It is not merely that we have actual experience of something better, although I believe that in fact to be the case; it is rather that we cannot be content without it. If we did not know a better system than over-all collectivism, we should have to create it. For in our generation we have seen the ghastly alternative—a mob of bemused slaves and prostitute intellectuals, mouthing the praises of the Great Dictator, an ultimate degradation of the type man.

[7] Mill, *On Liberty*, Blackwell Ed., pp. 99-100.

V

But how are we to conceive the desirable alternative, the system of diffused ownership and spontaneous enterprise? In popular discussion of these matters, it has become a habit to refer to such system as a system of *laissez faire*, thereby in my opinion, leading to endless confusion of thought and argument at cross purposes.

So far as its use in history is concerned, the term *laissez faire* has a great variety of meanings. Originally, it seems to have been a protest against paternalistic regulation. It was in this form that it was used by Le Gendre and Gournay; and it was in this form that it became one of the slogans of the popular free trade movements of the nineteenth century. Its development as the basis of a system was chiefly the work of the Physiocrats and certain nineteenth century continental writers —Bastiat is perhaps the most outstanding. But it was not used in this sense by the English Classical Economists. The word is only at all prominent in the work of John Stuart Mill and that in a context so hedged about by reservations that it would be quite absurd to identify his position with that of the real exponents of the let-alone philosophy. J. E. Cairnes, the last of the representatives of this tradition, in his essay on *Political Economy and Laissez Faire* expressly repudiated the whole outlook; while Marshall, eclectic as always, but a thousand miles from the continental *laissez faire* position, tried to give what he called "a new emphasis to the watch-word": "Let everyone work with all his might; and most of all let the government arouse itself to do that work which is vital and which none but government can do efficiently."[8] In recent years *laissez faire* has come to be used as a term of abuse, and totalitarian writers have not been slow to take advantage of this to stigmatize any policy whatever which in

[8] *Memorials of Alfred Marshall,* Ed. A. C. Pigou (1925), p. 336.

any way smacks of freedom. I await with virtual certainty the emergence of the term *laissez faire* collectivism to smear those socialist plans that would at least allow some freedom in the sphere of consumption.

Thus if we take the various historical usages of the term, we can make it mean more or less what we like; and there is no use in discussing it on this basis. Indeed, there would be much to be said for a compact, if it could be expected that it would be honourably observed by all parties, whereby use of the term disappeared from the vocabulary. Still, if we take it in the sense in which it was originally made the basis of a general system, if, that is to say, we take it as meaning a state of affairs in which the functions of the state are restricted to those of a night watchman and in which the law that is enforced consists in a very few simple prescriptions chiefly concerning property and contract, the rest being left to spontaneous co-operation guided by the market, then we can say that it stands for a conception differing very greatly from the conception of a liberal order that would be thought appropriate by those of us who follow the English Classical tradition, suitably modified to take account of the needs and the intellectual discoveries of this part of the twentieth century. It is true that both systems attach great importance to freedom as an objective. It is true that both systems depend upon recognition of the possibilities of order implicit in the institutions of property and the market. But their conceptions of the nature of this order and the functions of government necessary to bring it about are so different as to constitute two very different systems. Let me try to indicate what, in my judgment, are the main deficiencies of the systems, let us say, of Bastiat or Herbert Spencer, as regards the organization of production.

First, I would say, that a *laissez faire* system thus conceived, enormously underestimates, if it does not entirely ignore, the whole world of desirable state action that may be described as the provision of indiscriminate benefit. It is clear that it recognized the necessity for defence and a police force, and in Bastiat there are some references to what he calls the "common domain (Rivers, Forests, Roads)." But when we remember that Herbert Spencer even went so far as to oppose "State Ordered Drainage Systems,"[9] it is surely clear that the scope of state action in this respect was regarded as very restricted indeed. Personally, I think that both in regard to knowledge and to the general appearance of things there is still room in the twentieth century for considerable extensions of this kind of state activity. There are vast difficulties connected both with the endowment of research and with town and country planning, which in any extended treatment would require a section to themselves. But I do not think that recognition of the difficulties should preclude recognition of the strong arguments for action on quite a wide front.

Secondly, I think that this outlook almost entirely ignores the extent to which the intervention of the state is required even where the initiative in production is quite definitely in private or corporate hands. I am far from arguing that all forms of public utility regulation or franchises at present prevailing are necessary or even desirable—especially where statutory monopolies are created: current thought in this respect in my judgment is often very superficial. But it passes my comprehension to see how it could be thought that the provision of services involving long, continuous stretches of the earth's surface, excavation under public highways, regulation of the flow of large masses of water, and so on, could ever be carried to a desirable level without the special authorization and regulation by the State. Let us be quite clear about the quantitative significance of all this. If it be judged by the volume of investment it involves, I should guess that it must have absorbed at least a third of the savings of the last hundred

[9] *The Man versus the State* (1884), pp. 57-58.

and fifty years. Indeed, one of the most cogent arguments against general collectivism in my opinion is the argument that there is already so much that government cannot evade doing in this connection, that it is as well that it should concentrate its attention here and leave to other forms of organization, productive activities where such close association is not essential.

Thirdly, I suggest that the conceptions fostered by *laissez faire* both of property and of contract are altogether too simple—indeed, simple is not the word, *simpliste* is more appropriate. The idea that there are easily accessible clear archetypal concepts requiring a minimum of drafting ingenuity to be translated into legal instruments suitable for all times and places just does not fit the facts of life. So far as property is concerned, what are we to regard as immutable natural rights in regard, for instance, to mining rights, rivers, inventions, symphonies? The idea does not bear examination. As for contract, the belief that complete freedom should be the order of the day, including freedom to destroy freedom, is in contradiction to our fundamental principles. I am disposed to agree that a good deal that has been written about monopoly in recent literature is not only barren but also positively misleading—a good example of the danger of generalizing from rather half-baked mathematical models without referring to facts. But I still believe, as against Schumpeter and others, that there is a real monopoly problem in free societies, and that it is unwise to resign ourselves to doing nothing about it.

Finally, I think that this outlook completely side-steps all the tremendous and perplexing problems connected with the maintenance of aggregate demand. The theory of the market, as it has come down to us from Adam Smith, does indeed suggest that given reasonable stability of aggregate demand and an absence of monopolistic restriction, a system of markets and private property will turn out a flow of goods and services roughly corresponding to the demands of consumers and investors—a spontaneous order within the realm of freedom. But in itself it provides no guarantee that aggregate demand will be stable; expectations in that connection depend upon more complicated theoretical constructions. Now I am far from wishing to suggest that there can be no expectations of stability in this respect; that it is all a matter of fluke that the system is not always either at the zero or deflation or the infinity of hyper-inflation—some of us need occasionally to remind ourselves that the Great Depression was something unique in economic history. But I am quite sure that if we are in a position to expect satisfactory conditions in this respect, it must be in part at any rate the result of deliberate contrivance rather than predetermined harmony. There is no guarantee in the nature of things that just any spontaneous development in the sphere of money and credit will give us what we want. In fact I do not think we yet know nearly enough about these matters to be at all sure what are the best possible arrangements. But of one thing we can be fairly certain: whatever be the best institutions, whether they be 100 per cent money, free banking on the joint stock model, or the complicated provisions of the Federal Reserve System, they are not the product of spontaneous initiative uninfluenced by the legal system. Where money and credit are concerned, the idea of a simple natural order is not only not plausible, it is also positively absurd.

It would be waste of time to spend further powder and shot on the conceptions of pure *laissez faire*. Indeed at this time of day, it would perhaps be more appropriate not so much to point out where it was wrong but rather to draw attention to the respects in which it was magnificently right— for at least its advocates were believers in freedom, at least they understood the working of the market, at least they saw through the sophistries of some paternalistic systems. But I think it is worth while to have focused thus briefly the deficiencies of their outlook if only to show by way of contrast wherein I suppose the better one to consist. I hope what I have said in this connection will at least assure you that in my conception the system of economic freedom, as Marshall called it, is not a closed system laid up in heaven, so to speak, deducible from a few simple concepts and capable of being transcribed on a couple of tablets of stone, but an evolving system, part natural growth, part artifact, continually adapting itself or being adapted to new conditions and new knowledge, whose only main general criterion is that it tends towards freedom rather than away from it.

VI

But what about distribution? What order is implied here by the general outlook which I have tried to indicate. It is at this point that we encounter egalitarian views and are obliged to consider the claims of equality as opposed to liberty.

There is clearly a certain sense in which the idea of equality is essential to the idea of a free society. The idea of equality before the law, the idea that in its dealings with the citizens, whether positive or negative, the state does not discriminate between different persons similarly situated—that is surely one of the bedrock conceptions of any society that is to be truly free. It is no accident that the more totalitarian minded of our advisers are ceaselessly attacking the principle of nondiscrimination. A society in which similarly situated persons received different treatment according to their race, their colour, or their proximity to the governmental machine, would be a society in which different people had different degrees of freedom *vis-à-vis* the coercive apparatus. That would be contrary to our general principles.

But equality before the law and the administrative machine is one thing, equality in every respect relating to real income is quite another. In a society in which incentive and allocation depend on private enterprise and the market, a continuous redistribution of income and property in the interests of a pattern of equality, or something approximating to equality, is almost a contradiction in terms. Only in a society in which the disposition to work could be assumed to operate entirely independently of pecuniary considerations and in which it could be assumed that the allocation problem could be solved from the centre without unfreedom and inefficiency, would it be possible to make distribution completely independent of the value of work done and to allow no inequality due to inequality of accumulation and changes in capital values. We know from Russian experience that, even under the sternest collectivism, the attempt to eliminate inequality due to inequality of pay has completely broken down. If, for reasons that I have discussed already, we decide to rely on private property as a basis of dispersed initiative and freedom, we must be prepared to tolerate the existence of some inequality arising from this source also.

This does not mean, in my judgment, the exclusion of any kind of redistribution. I do not think that the principles of a free society exclude all measures for the relief of misfortune. I think the principle of compulsory contribution may be carried too far—to the sapping of independence and the undue burdening of the main body of the citizens. But, at least at this stage in the evolution of modern societies, I should regard such measures as part of the indispensable cement of social union and as conferring on most of us a positive satisfaction in the functions that are performed. Further I do not rule out, but rather welcome, various supplements to family provisions that do something to mitigate for young people the inequality of opportunity that necessarily arises from inequality of parental position. I think that in all these matters we have something to learn from an earlier generation who regarded such measures as provisional.[10] If we may entertain the hope that eventually the great body of the citizens will enjoy the equivalent of middle class incomes, we may surely assume that in such circumstances it would be desirable that they should assume middle class responsibility. But that, in the present position of most western societies, some provision of this sort is desirable and creative of greater eventual freedom I have absolutely no doubt at all.

Finally, I wish to make it clear that I see no objection in principle to some mitigations of inequality in the interests of greater freedom. It is easy to conceive of societies in which, either as a heritage of a feudal past or the accident of the forces of the market, wealth becomes so concentrated in a few hands as to be dangerous to the political freedom of the many. I am bound to say that I think that, so far as most modern democracies go, this danger has been greatly exaggerated—the boot is rather on the other leg: the democratic leveling instinct tends to dangerous inroads on the disposition to preserve and accumulate. But where the danger exists, there the general principles of freedom would make it right to deal with it. I also think that these same principles make expedient those forms of taxation of property passing at death that tend to the diffusion of property—something very different from the effects of much inheritance taxation at present, which tends to its dissipation.

But when all these exceptions have been made, I must insist that leveling measures as such are no part of the policy of liberty. The free society is not to be built on envy; a state founded on green-eye will not stand. The position of those who say, "let there be more equality even if it involves less wealth all round," is absolutely antithetical to the outook which I have tried to explain in this lecture.

[10] On this point, see the very powerful article, "The Rationale of the Social Services," by Mr. Walter Hagenbruch, *Lloyds Bank Review* (July 1953).

VII

One final word by way of elucidation. The picture that I have been trying to draw is essentially a picture of a society so organized that individual initiative is free without inflicting damage on others and collective action is directed to enhancing freedom rather than imposing a common pattern. Now it is fundamental to this conception that it depends upon law; that both individual and collective action should be based upon a knowledge of regulations laid down beforehand and generally applicable, rather than upon arbitrary edicts laid down to fit the circumstances of each particular case. The desirability of rules rather than authorities, to use the contrast posed so vividly by Henry Simons, is absolutely central to the main libertarian position.

Nevertheless I want to suggest that we deceive ourselves and oversimplify our position to a point at which we may expose it to ridicule, if we allow ourselves to think that all necessary rules can always be laid down in advance of the event and that nothing need be left to the discretion of legislatures and administrations. I think it is a deficiency of the libertarian case as it is often stated, that even when it explicitly repudiates the superficialities of extreme *laissez faire,* it tends to suggest a conception of government that is too limited to the execution of known laws, to the exclusion of functions of initiative and discretion that cannot without distortion be left out of the picture. That we should have as much of legal fixity and automatic control mechanism as possible is eminently to be desired. But that we need have *nothing* but this, that all that is done by government which is not covered by this definition is either mistaken or definitely illiberal—this I suggest is not a position that will sustain serious examination.

We may note at the outset that all that sphere of governmental activity which may be described as the provision of indiscriminate benefit is *ipso facto* removed from the sphere of possible automatism. How much there should be of flood control, of smoke prevention, of the provision of civic amenities, of national parks and so on, these are problems that cannot be settled by the application of known rules; they depend essentially upon specific acts of choice. Modern legislatures and modern administrators are confronted by the urgent necessity for very many such acts.

But beyond this, and well within the sphere in which, *other things being equal,* we should hope for the predominant operation of automatic adjustment mechanisms, there are all sorts of contingencies, not in the least to be regarded as impossible, that interrupt the simplicity of the picture and call for special intervention or initiative. Take for instance the sphere of finance. Even if we were dealing with an absolutely closed community, it would surely be unwise, in the present state of knowledge, to assume that no situation could arise that could not be dealt with by purely automatic mechanisms; while if we are dealing with the affairs of open communities in a world of states each capable of pursuing divergent policies, I submit that it would be pure lunacy to argue that nothing could happen that could not be dealt with by pre-established stabilizers. Suppose, for instance, that some powerful state set itself, not only to absorb all the increase of gold supply but also to draw to itself by deliberate deflation all the gold already in existence. Would any responsible person be prepared to argue that the other governments should stand by with their hands crossed, confident that in the long run either the offending state would get sick of the price it had to pay, or that their own citizens would spontaneously evolve habits for dealing with a continuously shrinking volume of aggregate expenditure?

It may be said, however, that finance is in a class by itself. I admit that it offers some of the most obvious examples for the case I am trying to make. But I am afraid it does not by any means exhaust the field of possibilities. We all know that quite apart from the provision of military forces and weapons (which perhaps can be brought under the heading of indiscriminate benefit) the fact of war, or sometimes merely near war, necessitates the application of controls cutting right across the normal reaction mechanism of private enterprise and markets. So, too, may postwar demobilization. But war and its accompaniments are not the only circumstances calling for extraordinary interventions. It is true that many of such circumstances arise because of the policies of other states—subsidy policies, state trading, and other such maneuvers; to the extent that we eventually succeed in getting international affairs more subject to a commonly agreed set of rules, such contingencies would not arise. But even if we are thinking of that remote abstraction—a world state or federation, it is not at all difficult to think of occasions when governmental action in supplement to or replacement of the ordinary forces of production and distribution would be called for. I will not rely on the time-honored example of acts of God—natural disasters. To make the position clear, I am quite prepared to admit that I can easily think of inventions or even changes of taste that might produce such a situation. A discovery rendering rapidly valueless the product of populations unused to migration would fall into this category. I would say that in such circumstances it is quite possible that some intervention is desirable, if only to preserve the solidarity and coherence of the free society.

It may be argued that such an admission is dangerous, that once it is conceded that the mere fact of change may give rise to circumstances justifying the creation of controls other than the controls of the market and the legal framework, we have opened the floodgates to any sort of folly, and there is no longer any difference between our position and the position of pure interventionist opportunism. I admit the danger. But I cannot accept the implication that we should deny the facts of life and pretend that such circumstances are inconceivable. Modern liberals who appear to suggest that *everything* can be reduced to rules and automatic control mechanisms and that politics can be left to second-raters and nitwits do not make their main case more plausible. On the contrary they run the danger of bringing it into undeserved discredit.

Moreover, to admit that cases of this sort are conceivable is not to imply that they are always likely to occur; probably most of the instances of alleged distress caused by change are best left to the existing apparatus of general relief. Nor does it imply that all kinds of measures to deal with them are equally justifiable. On the contrary, it is just at this point that the general point of view that I have been trying to develop comes into its own again as a guide to policy. That is to say, we must distinguish between interventions that destroy the need for intervention and interventions that tend to prepetuate it; and it is only the former that are admissible. In the example that I have cited I should say that measures designed to promote mobility from the stricken area were an example of the former kind of intervention, while measures designed to suppress the invention that caused the trouble or to subsidize the price of the affected product were an example of the latter. For although with the first type of intervention, the policy adopted would tend to remove the fundamental disequilibrium, the second would tend to prolong it and even perhaps to provoke other interventions. Here as elsewhere, with all acts of government, the final test is always whether the control imposed is in the service of freedom or in the service of some other conception of society.

May I end with a quotation that will take us back to the ethical ultimates from which I started. Most of you will remember the fine lines that Dr. Johnson inserted at the end of Oliver Goldsmith's *Traveller:*

> In every government though terrors reign,
> Though tyrant kings, or tyrant laws restrain,
> How small, of all that human hearts endure,
> That part which laws or kings can cause or cure.

I do not think that students of society in the twentieth century can go all the way with this. We know that modern technique has made it possible for tyrant kings or tyrant gangs to create a hell permeating almost all sections of society; and we believe we know the institutions that make such catastrophes less probable. We hope too that our analysis indicates some forms of social order that may release forces capable of going far to diminish the worst evils of disease and poverty. But if Dr. Johnson's lines serve to remind us that the goal of all such efforts is chiefly negative—to reduce evil rather than create good—and that when everything has been done in the sphere of desirable organization:

> Still to ourselves in every place consigned,
> Our own felicity we make or find

they will still be salutary. For it is the essence of the libertarian outlook that where the true positive goods of life begin, there the economist and the political philosopher must bow and take their leave; for in that sphere they have nothing to do.